Financial Times Briefings

FT Prentice Hall
FINANCIAL TIMES

In an increasingly competitive world, we believe it's quality of thinking that gives you the edge – an idea that opens new doors, a technique that solves a problem, or an insight that simply makes sense of it all. The more you know, the smarter and faster you can go.

That's why we work with the best minds in business and finance to bring cutting-edge thinking and best learning practice to a global market.

Under a range of leading imprints, including *Financial Times Prentice Hall*, we create world-class print publications and electronic products bringing our readers knowledge, skills and understanding, which can be applied whether studying or at work.

To find out more about Pearson Education publications, or tell us about the books you'd like to find, you can visit us at **www.pearsoned.co.uk**

STEPHEN HOARE
and
ANDREW LEIGH

Financial Times Briefing on
Talent Management

**Financial Times
Prentice Hall
is an imprint of**

Harlow, England • London • New York • Boston • San Francisco • Toronto • Sydney • Singapore • Hong Kong
Tokyo • Seoul • Taipei • New Delhi • Cape Town • Madrid • Mexico City • Amsterdam • Munich • Paris • Milan

PEARSON EDUCATION LIMITED

Edinburgh Gate
Harlow CM20 2JE
Tel: +44(0)1279 623623
Fax: +44(0)1279 431059
Website: www.pearsoned.co.uk

First published in Great Britain in 2011

ISBN: 978-0-273-73639-4

British Library Cataloguing-in-Publication Data
A catalogue record for this book is available from the British Library

Library of Congress Cataloging-in-Publication Data
A catalog record for this book is available from the Library of Congress

10 9 8 7 6 5 4 3 2 1
15 14 13 12 11

Typeset in 9.25 Swiss 721 BT by 30
Printed by Ashford Colour Press Ltd, Gosport

FAST ANSWERS TO CRITICAL BUSINESS DECISIONS

As a high-performance leader you need to tackle pressing business issues and deliver hard measurable results. *Financial Times Briefings* give you the targeted advice you need to:

- get to grips with business critical issues quickly
- develop a solutions-focused mindset
- ask the right questions
- take the right actions
- measure the right things
- make the right decisions.

Key features include:

- Clear, concise information
- A focus on actions and objectives rather than theory
- Brief, relevant case studies of success stories and failures
- Benchmarks and metrics to gauge outcomes and achievements
- Briefing lessons to distil key business insights

Financial Times Briefings *series advisors:*

- Jim Champy, author of bestselling business book *Reengineering the Corporation* and Chairman Emeritus, Consulting, Dell Services
- Rob Grimshaw, Managing Director of FT.com
- David MacLeod, co-author of the MacLeod report on employee engagement and non-executive director at MOJ and DfID
- John Mullins, Professor at London Business School
- Sir Eric Peacock, non-executive board member with UKTI and a board member of the Foreign and Commonwealth Office Public Diplomacy Board
- Kai Peters, CEO of Ashridge Business School
- Simon Waldman, Group Product Director at LOVEFiLM

Praise for *Financial Times Briefing on Talent Management*

'Talent Management is extremely important to Marriott hotels and we invest strongly in it. This new book by Stephen Hoare and Andrew Leigh will be helpful to anyone wanting to gain an understanding of the nature of talent management and how to go about making it happen. Clearly written with plenty of examples and practical advice.'

Robert Gary Dodds, Vice President Human Resources, Marriott International Inc. & Ritz Carlton Hotel Company, Middle East & Africa Continent.

'This clear and highly readable book highlights the need for organisations and human resources professionals to be "talent-minded". It delivers practical hints and tips for implementing a talent strategy aligned to business direction. An essential holistic text for any professional working within talent, blending both business and psychological perspectives.'

Elouise Leonard-Cross, Leadership and Talent Manager, Home Group Ltd

'This book looks at talented people and peak performance. Does the peak performer combine self belief, high order skills and the capacity to trust themselves to read situations, – to "get into the zone"? Replicating high level performance is a challenge to each of us and this book helped me think this through.'

Colin Carnall, Chief Executive, CassExec, City University

'This book is now the only one you need on talent management. It synthesises all the relevant theories in an interesting and ultimately entertaining way and adds the author's own perspective to provide a genuinely good read while simultaneously delivering a full reference capability.'

Chris Brady, Dean, BPP Business School

Acknowledgements

We are grateful to the following for permission to reproduce copyright material:

Figure 3.2 adapted from Figure 3, 'Stages of Development of Talent Strategy' in 'Talent: Strategy Management Measurement', CIPD 2007, p.16; table on p.107 reprinted courtesy of PricewaterhouseCoopers; Figure 8.1 adapted from Figure 9, 'The Talent Perspective' in 'The Talent Perspective: What does it feel like to be talent managed?', CIPD 2010, p.185; table on p.141 from 'Leveraging the Talent-Driven Organization', Richard Adler, rapporteur, The Aspen Institute, 2010. Reproduced with permission.

In some instances we have been unable to trace the owners of copyright material, and we would appreciate any information that would enable us to do so.

Contents

[PART ONE]

In brief

Executive summary

1

Introduction

Across the globe organisations are increasingly talent-driven. It will probably be another decade, though, before we fully recognise the true nature of this global phenomenon. And it is unlikely we will still talk about talent management, engagement or unlocking people's potential. Almost certainly, a decade on, those who have not embraced such factors that are determining organisational success will no longer be in the race.

Efficiency, size, profits, shareholder interests and, above all, scale, all drove 20th-century organisations. They provided a rationale that at the time seemed to make commercial sense. Yet these factors are becoming far less significant in determining what a successful company looks like. There are different forces at work that often leave today's giant corporations looking like slow-moving dinosaurs, finding it hard to adapt to the new realities.

In the previous century the old imperative for businesses was to keep getting bigger, so as to achieve scalable efficiencies. Mergers and acquisitions became a way of life. These seem decidedly dated now in their consistent failure to deliver expected business benefits and their tendency to destroy shareholder value. With the emerging digital infrastructure force feeding the pace of change, a strategy based on size makes far less sense.

Size creates inflexibility and less leverage for innovation. What once was championed as a core strength, forward-thinking leaders and managers now see as a core rigidity. Or as one senior executive has emotively described it: 'What made us successful is now killing us.'

The centrality of talent to 21st-century organisations makes them different to their predecessors. Rather than scale, what matters more is the ability to problem solve, be creative and innovative, and generate a culture of continual improvement. The focus of how to run a successful corporation is therefore shifting, almost as we watch, towards those who can help deliver such a culture. The pace is relentless, and many astute organisations are diligently transforming themselves into places where learning, not size, is becoming core to the business, and where communication and collaboration produce new solutions for customers.

Executives responsible for the direction of organisations are therefore turning to their brightest people to help with this change and the implications for talent's role are only gradually emerging. One concern is that talent has knock-on effects as to how we view the nature of successful leadership.

Finding your successor was always some part of a senior manager's concern. But today that is translating into a far more prominent part of virtually every leader's job description. Some might even argue that it is becoming a leader's number one priority. But such a view has not always held sway.

The traditional ideal of leadership is based on a romantic notion that it must be macho and decisive. It also took as its imagery the man on the white charger saving a company: most notably Victor Kiam, who liked Remington razors so much he bought the company; Lee Iacocca who rescued Chrysler, albeit temporarily, to universal acclaim; and more recently Carly Fiorina winning and losing the role of white knight at Hewlett-Packard.

This exaggerated view of leadership has led to celebrating the larger-than-life magnate, the supreme individual. Today's hall of fame – Richard Branson, Bill Gates, Rupert Murdoch, Lakshmi Mittal, Philip Green and Martin Sorrell – are recognisably the same buccaneering breed as past moguls such as Rockefeller, Andrew Carnegie, Randolph Hearst and Cornelius Vanderbilt.

Despite these high-profile winners, many rather less exalted CEOs of global businesses have come to the fore due to careful and successful succession planning. As one of the most insightful leadership studies of the late 20th century showed,[1] leaders who run highly successful long-standing organisations are defined by duality – they are modest yet wilful, humble yet fearless. And above all, they have a deep and abiding understanding of the importance of talent, while not necessarily articulating it in quite that way.

With the world of business increasingly global and ever more connected, entire economic hot spots now act as cultural melting pots, with a cadre of international executives – literally top talent – moving freely between cities like Mumbai, New York, London, Frankfurt and Dubai.

In this febrile and constantly evolving landscape leadership is being redefined as less macho and more consensual, democratic and inclusive. New leaders and their organisations recognise the unique contribution individuals bring to the table, rather than regarding their workers as faceless drones.

Far more is being expected of leaders in the way they relate to other human beings. Where once remoteness and hierarchies held sway, we now expect 21st-century leaders to show high levels of emotional intelligence, to know how to nurture talent, and to pursue the inescapable logic of flattening organisational structures.

Those who fail to respond to the imperative to create a talent-driven organisation are liable to lead their organisations into the wilderness. For example, the length of time a big corporation can expect to stay up with the winners has fallen from 75 years in 1934 to just 15 years in 2010.

As part of this shift to the talent-driven organisation in which a new form of leadership holds sway, there is a wider recognition that employees need to do far more than just turn up for work. Instead, there is a demand for high levels of engagement, in which people act almost as volunteers, willingly 'going the extra mile', putting in what the occupational psychologists describe as 'discretionary effort'.

The trouble is, globally companies are generally a long way from understanding the importance of engagement and the role it plays in influencing a host of key variables from profitability to customer satisfaction, from higher retention rates to better sales.

And while top management in many companies say that managing talent is important, the reality is that far too many employees remain frustrated and alienated by what happens at their workplace. Practices that were hardly noticed in the

[1] Jim Collins (2001) *Good to Great,* Random House.

20th-century firm are now recognised as curtailing the freedom of the individual and driving away the most creative high-performing employees. Significantly, the bigger the company the lower the levels of engagement amongst staff.

Thus we are seeing command and control, which may have served organisations well in the past, being rapidly consigned to history. It may once have been the preferred and comfortable style of many managers yet it leaves little room to discover what each person regards as meaningful work, or what would make them feel excited and passionate about their contribution.

The previous management practice that took talent for granted, seeing it as a fixed resource and limited to mainly the best and the brightest, is being increasingly challenged. Instead, the demand is for ways to tap into the potential of every employee and assume that each has something unique to offer that can be discovered and exploited.

Turbulent times have thrown a spotlight on talent as never before. Managing it is probably closer to how a successful repertory theatre company operates in bringing together talent to perform briefly and then to disband and reform for a new venture. As the influential US Aspen Institute puts it:

Instead of depending on the ability of a few 'lone heroes', the success of the 21st-century firm is built on the effectiveness of multiple high performance teams, some of which may exist only long enough to take on and solve a particular problem and may involve people outside as well as inside the firm.[2]

This performance-based culture raises all kinds of questions for practising executives, particularly how they can exercise their influence. One answer is that talent needs to be seen as abundant rather than scarce. The old 'war for talent' is rapidly being recognised for the sham that it always was. Of course there are shortages in specific skills, but the reality is that behind every single leader are many talented people at all levels, all contributing to the overall success of their organisations.

Rather than treating talent as a scarce resource new leadership skills demand the ability to find talent everywhere, to 'unlock people's potential'. By learning how to encourage people to be the best they can everyone becomes a winner.

To sum up the purpose of this book, it is to explain that organisations are increasingly talent-driven, that engagement lies at the core of exploiting talent and that the requirement to find and manage talent is changing the role of leaders. These are factors that will almost certainly challenge even the most enlightened executive.

What, for example, will it mean for your organisation to become truly talent-driven, and how might you go about making that happen? Or having accepted the importance of engagement to your organisation's success, what steps can you take to alter these levels in both macro and micro terms? Or if the changes

[2] Richard Adler (rapporteur) (2010) 'Leveraging the Talent-Driven Organization', Communications and Society Program, The Aspen Institute.

that being a talent-driven organisation imply are duly followed through, what will it mean for your personal leadership and those of your colleagues?

We have tried to answer these questions throughout the rest of this book using the overarching theme of talent management. As you will already be aware, this concept is something of a moveable feast, with no universal definition of either talent or the respective processes that constitute a talent management system.

You will have to decide on both, but hopefully the contents of this book will provide a sufficient route map to help you make some viable decisions for your organisation. What is certain is that talent management demands both a macro response in the form of a definite strategy, and a micro one in the form of a focus on individuals and what they need in order to deliver outstanding performance.

In the case of strategy this must be resolved at the most senior level in your organisation if it is to be coherent, effective and ultimately transparent. The strategy needs to reflect the external environment in which your organisation operates and should therefore be as inclusive as possible.

In reviewing talent management strategies we have encountered no sure-fire solutions that apply to every situation, other than that the pursuit of commercial priorities and investment in people are not mutually exclusive. Each organisation must work out its own route to becoming talent-driven and what that means in practice.

Many companies and organisations are already on the right track. Their leaders are learning to develop a mix and match of talent management policies that suits the needs and priorities of their particular organisation and where it is in the development cycle. Some may start out on the talent management journey while others have already developed quite sophisticated strategies that can be applied to their organisations on a grand scale.

If there is no one size fits all approach to talent management, we do know that organisation structure, roles and responsibilities play a big part in how it is turned into a reality. Every leader, every executive and every supervisor is their own talent manager, with a responsibility to find and make the best use of talent around them.

Even if you agree that your organisation should be talent-driven so as to remain relevant in the 21st century, you and your colleagues may be less sure how to move from the present structure to a new one. As the Aspen Institute observes:

> *the reality is that it is almost antithetical to the values of many corporate cultures to create an environment that encourages risk-taking and continuous innovation; to support transparency and open engagement with suppliers, partners, customers; and to create conditions that maximise opportunities for continuous learning throughout the firm.*[3]

Google's 'innovation time off', where employees spend up to 20% of their time on their own innovation projects or ideas has been one high-profile solution to creating

[3] Ibid.

the right environment for change. But there are many others and you are only limited by your imagination as to what will do it for your own organisation.

What will not work is sticking to the old-style approach in which leaders make decisions and tell people what to do to carry out them out. In a world getting ever more complex, decision making by leaders alone is almost bound to fail. The only sure way to make the right choices is the dual strategy of encouraging lots of experiments, while tapping into the collective wisdom of talent across and beyond the company.

In moving towards a talent-driven organisation you will almost certainly encounter considerable inertia. This is par for the course for any change programme, but that does not mean the change cannot be made. It does, however, mean becoming aware of just what it takes to shift organisational culture and to sustain the changes once they have been made. It also means shifting away from what worked in the past so as to respond to the live challenges of the moment. For example, how will your organisation gain fresh perspectives and new skills? As one senior executive has put it: 'the company's collective IQ should increase with every new hire'.

On a personal level, you may wonder where to start in pursuing the whole talent management issue and again we have tried to show ways in which you might approach this task. But inevitably what we are really doing is raising awareness. What may be reassuring is that people in your organisation and outside it may well have some sound ideas to offer you and in that sense your journey need not be a solitary one.

Certainly in a complex and rapidly changing environment it is hard to design and implement an ideal solution to talent management. If your organisation is to remain agile with a culture that values talent then look for signs that it is constantly experimenting and providing experiences for employees that allow them to grow and fulfil their potential. As we say elsewhere in the book, if you grow your people, you will certainly grow the company.

Why should you read this book?

You should read this book to find out how talent management can help you engage your people. By investing in them and by helping them develop, you are making them and your organisation more productive.

As we explain, talent management is not about the select few. It is what an organisation does to recruit, retain and develop talent for its future benefit. It is linked closely to strategy, organisational culture and change management.

Ownership of the talent management strategy must take place at board level if it is to be coherent and effective. This strategy needs to reflect the external environment in which the company or organisation operates and should therefore be inclusive. Talent management policies covering recruitment, development and retention, and remuneration of staff should be fair, open and transparent. Talent management is not something that is done to people; it is something to which everyone should feel a part of.

As one of the talent directors we interviewed for this book told us: 'Commercial priorities and investment in people is not an either/or.' Talent management policies in the shape of recruitment, training, performance management and appraisal and succession planning may be costly to implement. But the benefits in the shape of enhanced employee engagement, business productivity, creativity and morale far outweigh the costs.

To make the business case, the effects of talent management policies should be measurable and verifiable: in an ideal world! Of course, many talent managers understand the subtle but tangible impact of culture on morale.

 Briefing lessons

- **Talent management dovetails with business strategy; it is a driver of employee engagement and is an aspect of change management.**
- **Talent-powered organisations are agile; they find it easy to adapt to changing economic circumstances.**
- **Every leader, every executive and every supervisor is their own talent manager, with a responsibility to find and make the best use of talent around them.**
- **The aim of talent management is to create an environment that encourages risk taking and continuous innovation. It supports transparency and open engagement with suppliers, partners and customers, and maximises opportunities for continuous learning throughout the firm.**

What is talent management?

2

Introduction

The CEO of the Indian IT services giant HCL has a bracing motto: 'employee first, customer second'. Yet Vineet Nayar is no flaky idealist. His company has 55,000 staff with a market capitalisation of $24 billion. Looking after employees and making the most of their talent is not just a 'nice to have' for Nayar, but a way of life. It helps explain much of his success in getting the best from his people.[1]

CEOs around the world often talk glibly in the abstract about talent. They explain they think talent is 'a good thing' and should be nurtured. But what exactly do they really mean by talent?

In fashion, for example, 'talent' refers to the high priests of couture like Christian Dior and Vivienne Westwood. In football, premier league strikers are the 'the talent' while down at the pub it may be a crude euphemism for someone's sexual appeal. In financial services, talent acquires yet another meaning, with top-end hedge managers and investment bankers vacuuming up astronomical bonuses on the often dubious grounds that they really deserve it.

In our achievement and celebrity driven society, talent tends to sit on a pedestal for the rest of us to gape at, underpinned with a heavy dose of admiration or envy. We lavish talent with star treatment, regarding those who have it as somehow different, exceptional, an elite.

Viewing talent as a rare commodity severely limits the amount of talent available to any one company. This unashamedly elitist approach may lead to treating your workforce as having little value compared to the shiny nuggets of the elite.

Yet how limited is talent? Is the job of managers merely to find the gold nuggets, polish them and then hand them on to a grateful company?

Talent is not nearly as rare as you might think. Given the chance, just about every employee has the capability to demonstrate some kind of talent, the ability to make a difference in their particular area of work.

Realising that talent is spread throughout the organisation leads astute CEOs to be people-minded in their leadership. What drives organisations like Nayar's to high performance is not necessarily skill in financial markets, mergers and acquisitions or deal making. Instead, competitive advantage lies deep inside the company and is based on its people. And given the challenges facing the fast-growing organisation this has to mean all the people, not just a few of them.

The need to make the best use of talent, either as a rare resource or as a widely available one, has evolved into the current idea of 'talent management'. We are not talking about talent in the abstract. Our view is that it can help drive and transform the organisation to achieve exceptional performance.

As an activity and an idea, talent management is relevant across the organisational spectrum from private to public sector, from charities to NGOs and the armed forces. For all of them, talent matters and an important job of all managers is ensuring it delivers.

[1] P. Capelli and others (2010) 'Leadership lessons from India', *Harvard Business Review*, March.

Definitions of talent management vary. Some confuse talent management with employee engagement, a sub-set of talent management, and the outcome of a talent management policy is alignment across a number of organisational areas.

Talent management can also be defined by what it isn't. It does *not* cover basic HR functions, such as payroll or industrial relations.

 Definition

Talent management: what an organisation does to recruit, retain and develop talent for its future benefit. It is linked closely to strategy, organisational culture and change management.

Developing a strategy

According to workplace engagement specialists Best Companies, talent management strategy is decided at board level in most organisations. This was corroborated by a 2009 Maynard Leigh report, *Talent Management at the Crossroads,* which found that this was the case in three-quarters of companies questioned.

No two company talent management strategies will be the same, because priorities may range from the need to develop succession planning to boosting creativity to building capacity. The most effective talent management strategies are likely to be those that are bespoke, transparent, easy to understand and closely aligned with the needs of the business.

The point of adopting a talent management approach is its ability to focus attention on what the organisation needs to do to achieve high levels of performance and influence its future. Unlike old style HR, today's talent management is strategic. It is entirely future facing, even when making sure that today's talent is being fully exploited.

Talent management is an inescapable job of every executive at every level. It does not matter whether you work all day with machines or columns of figures or do not even have a team to direct. If you are a manager then, in essence, you must deal with people and this implies being concerned with success and getting the best out of the people you deal with, inspiring and encouraging them to go the extra mile and finding the next generation of leaders from the biggest possible gene pool. Broadly, talent management includes:

- recruitment
- performance management
- career development
- succession planning
- employee engagement processes.

These processes make up a cycle of activities. The point of talent management is bringing together these processes to raise bottom line profitability.

Talent-minded organisations recognise that while these processes may be supported by HR professionals they are essentially what all managers and leaders must master if they are to make a difference.

In this book, we take the view that talent management is an inclusive process. It is not just about filling roles but about engaging everyone in the company to make a contribution to improving themselves, their career prospects and job satisfaction, and by extension contributing to improved business performance.

Talent management is a consistent and joined-up approach to getting the best from people. It is a frame of mind in which the company invests in its people, and helps them develop their potential, their skills and their performance. Investment in talent and realigning the priorities of the company are a way of boosting creativity, productivity and the quality of service.

The war for talent

A ground-breaking report in 1999 by consultants McKinsey famously coined the phrase 'war for talent'. Since then, this evocative phrase has partly framed the managerial practices of talent management. At least one and possibly two generations of managers have come to believe that they are engaged in a war for talent that they must win at all costs. Such war imagery has bounced many employers into treating talent as a special case. This means paying a hefty premium to recruit and retain talent and from this has come the feeling that it is also synonymous with excess, pampering, spoiling and in some cases bribery.

In true McKinsey tradition, many organisations still refer to talent as a rare commodity. In their anxiety to retain it, sometimes little regard is paid to the true worth of the individuals singled out as the stars. The BBC, for example, refers to its top performers as talent. This includes stars like the now departed Jonathan Ross whose £18 million contract came to symbolise a spendthrift culture of unashamed elitism.

In 2010 the BBC published figures for the pay deals awarded to its so-called talent. According to reports, for instance, *Doctor Who* newcomer Matt Smith was stated to receive £1 million over the next five years. Nor is it just actors who are regarded as talent. In 2009 the BBC's own management salary list topped £14.3 million with the corporation's director pulling in £647,000 a year and others, like the deputy director, around half a million pounds.

Traditionally, the narrow definition of talent as focused only on high potentials links to divisive policies such as paying bonuses to senior managers and offering perks and benefits to the favoured few. This narrow approach is out of line with employee engagement and ignores the contribution talent can make at all levels of the organisation. To make sense of the war for talent it hardly helps that some organisations continue to use 'talent' as shorthand for their rising stars or future leaders while others regard all their employees as having talent.

What is often forgotten is that talent does not flourish in a vacuum. For individual talent to succeed usually requires supportive teamwork and an environment with appropriate HR structures that allow the stars to shine. The evidence from long-term successful organisations now strongly points to the inescapable fact that everyone in a company has a part to play in the drama of getting the best from people. There may indeed be bit part players, those with walk-on roles and others with more than just a few lines to say. Yet how they do this can make or break the organisation's overall performance. As they say in the acting profession, there are no small parts, only small actors.

In rejecting the war for talent concept we are not of course denying the reality of shortfalls in specific skill areas or in demographic trends such as an ageing population or the shrinking supply of 35–44-year-olds, particularly in the US.

Shifts in where people want to work also create temporary shortfalls in skill availability. To those on the receiving end, talent indeed seems in short supply. Around a third of recently qualified MBAs in America, for example, preferred to work for a start-up or a small business. Similarly the proportion of computer science and electrical engineering graduates who choose to go to smaller companies rather than established ones has risen to 37% from 22% in the 1980s. These are not shortfalls so much as career choices.

Context

The context in which many managers operate is that their organisations are competing for resources, markets and talent. They must secure human capital as part of survival and growth and for many this means trying to obtain more than their fair share of what is available.

The context can also be complex, unpredictable and even bizarre. Making sense of it requires an appreciation of some of the important influences at work, especially in the demand and supply of talent. For example, according to Cambridge University researchers, testosterone levels amongst city traders are higher on days when they make more than their average profit. Over the Channel, French Business School Ceram reports that the fewer female managers a company employs the more its share price is likely to fall.

A 2010 CIPD study[2] identified four basic contexts in which talent managers must operate: external, organisational, employers and the workforce (see Figure 2.1).

[2] CIPD (2010) 'Talent Management: An Overview', revised edition, July.

Figure 2.1 Demand, supply and context factors for talent management

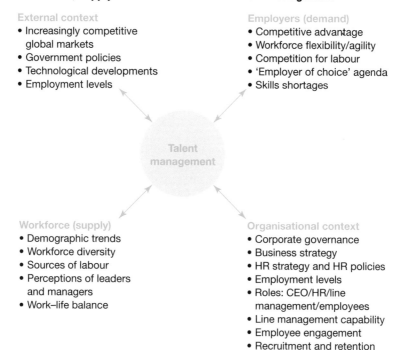

External context
- Increasingly competitive global markets
- Government policies
- Technological developments
- Employment levels

Employers (demand)
- Competitive advantage
- Workforce flexibility/agility
- Competition for labour
- 'Employer of choice' agenda
- Skills shortages

Talent management

Workforce (supply)
- Demographic trends
- Workforce diversity
- Sources of labour
- Perceptions of leaders and managers
- Work–life balance

Organisational context
- Corporate governance
- Business strategy
- HR strategy and HR policies
- Employment levels
- Roles: CEO/HR/line management/employees
- Line management capability
- Employee engagement
- Recruitment and retention
- Succession planning

Source: See note 2.

External context

We are seeing unprecedented change in reshaping the workplace almost beyond recognition. Just a decade ago, who could have confidently predicted the sustained rise of virtual working, an upsurge in concerns about diversity, a growing obsession with sustainability or the boom in self-employment?

The dotcom boom at the end of the 1990s saw an explosion in internet use, video conferencing, wikis and social networking, all of which is transforming where and how talent can work. These new layers of complexity pose new challenges for understanding how to adapt one's style and approach to talent management.

Technology allows a growing proportion of people to select their place of work, whether working from a home office or on the move. One implication is that employers can access new and underutilised talent pools. This now includes people with minor disabilities, parents caring for young children or dependants at home, even people prepared to work fewer hours in the cause of achieving a better work–life balance.

In globalised companies, talent managers often deal with change on an epic scale. It may now involve, for instance, co-ordinating virtual teams operating in different countries, conducting appraisals across regions, or creating an organisation-wide culture with a common set of values.

The rise of the BRIC economies – Brazil, Russia, India and China – and the oil rich Gulf States and Far East have added a further twist to globalisation and what this means for getting the best from people or finding talent in the first place. In the economic hot spots of Shanghai, Mumbai, Singapore and Dubai, for instance, the now firmly established new breed of footloose capitalism operates across national boundaries.

Such forces have numerous consequences including creating a new strain of expatriate. This is mobile talent on a short-term contract and drawn from many nationalities. Fluent in English, and kitted out with gold standard qualifications such as the totemic MBA, this is now a rarefied cadre of talent able to flit from country to country. Understanding and managing this talent demands a whole new set of assumptions about what will unlock such people's potential.

Even in the context of smaller regional or local companies, there are important changes in employment law covering areas such as working time, equality, age and gender – all issues that combine to make managing talent a complex and challenging task.

Workforce context

'Too many companies are wasting their resources' claimed an insightful report[3] on the use of talent in 2007, and it is fair to assume this continues today. The financial crisis has added urgency to the need for talent management to find a new approach to increasing employee engagement, beyond mere financial reward. Getting the commitment of employees needed in a crunch situation is becoming a major concern of companies.

As a senior learning and development manager of a global engineer and design company based partly in Dubai told us: 'We do all these surveys on staff commitment and engagement but frankly we do not do much with the results.'

Studies of employees expressing loyalty to employers are all too revealing. One US study in 2008 showed loyalty plummeting from 95% to 39% and the number trusting their employers falling just as dramatically from 79% to 22% over the same period. The level of disenchantment with the workplace and the employer continued into mid-2009 and possibly beyond.

Changing demographics are causing dramatic shifts in the makeup of the workforce. Age, or rather generational change, now presents a significant factor to consider in managing talent, with competition for younger workers likely to become more intense. This is not just a UK phenomenon. Elsewhere, lower birth rates and declining population size are similarly starting to generate pressures on the labour supply as a whole.

[3] DeAnne Aguirre and others (2009) 'The Talent Innovation Imperative', Autumn, reprint 09304, Booze & Co.

Diversity

Diversity too now plays a sizeable role in workplace management, stemming partly from legislation, but also from the ongoing competitive search for talent. More organisations now recognise that their survival depends on becoming proactive in attracting talent from a wider source than previously.

In June 2002, the then CEO of BP, Lord Browne, explained in stark terms why he was compelled to pursue the diversity issue:

> *The people we have form our human capital. To me that is a more important corporate asset than all the plant and equipment, all the oil fields and pipelines. If we can get a disproportionate share of the most talented people in the world, we have a chance of holding a competitive edge. That is the simple strategic logic behind our commitment to diversity and to the inclusion of individuals – men and women regardless of background, religion, ethnic origin, nationality or sexual orientation.*[4]

Other companies too see clearly the benefits of exploiting diversity. For example, pressure to use the talents of older people continues to grow. Companies like B&Q are charting new routes to employing and training older staff: one in four of its 3800 employers are aged over 50.

Johnson & Johnson: Crossing the finishing line

Johnson & Johnson (J&J) has identified high-performing black women as 'a pivotal group and successfully piloted an initiative aimed at accelerating their career development'.

The initiative, called Crossing the Finish Line, creates action plans with newly trained supervisors. According to J&J's chief diversity officer it 'helps us capitalise on talent that is reflected in the global environment and is different from the traditional mould'.

Source: DeAnne Aguirre and others (2009) 'The Talent Innovation Imperative',
Autumn reprint 09304, Booze and Co.

Trends that are forcing managers to seek talent from wherever they can find it include:

● demographic shifts: fewer younger people are available to recruit
● move to a knowledge economy: people increasingly feel able to vote with their feet if they are not treated well

---

[4] Lord Browne speaking at the Women in Leadership conference on 19 June 2002, Berlin.

- complexity of organisations: reliance on expertise and know-how
- knowledge limitations: a manager or leader can no longer know enough of how things work to single-handedly solve problems and make effective decisions
- cultural expectation: organisations are expected to play their part in contributing positively to society.

Just as an ecosystem's biological diversity increases its stability and productivity so cultural diversity brings together the resources and talents of many people for the shared benefit of all.

This greater openness towards diversity has a long way to go in many companies, particularly when it comes to drawing on the talents of certain ethnic groups and women. Ethnic groups as a whole tend to be under-represented in all professions and at all levels in both society and organisations. This has implications for the ability to tap into what is a rich source of talent readily available at a time when many companies are complaining about 'the war for talent'.

Women, who make up over half of undergraduates at UK universities, also have a raw deal. They are under-represented at the top of organisations, while being over-represented in lower levels, with a tendency to hit a glass ceiling in mid-career. In the Fortune 500 companies, female executives leave at twice the rate of men because they become frustrated with their work environment. This attrition rate is not merely a waste of talent, it also creates expensive replacement costs.

Women and minorities face great challenges both in entering and moving up in organisations. Even in BP Lord Browne had to admit that:

> In 1999 when we started on our current journey, just 8% of our top team – our top 450 people – were women. Of the top 40 – the Executive and Group Vice Presidents who run the company – none were women. Just 9% of the top team came from countries other than the US or the UK.[5]

Ensuring the talent pool is suitably diverse may be hard for managers to achieve on their own. But being aware of the dangers of lack of diversity and being willing to raise it as an issue can be an important contribution to more effective talent management practices in a company.

Demographics and Gen Y

As the baby boomers of the 1960s begin to retire, there is a new breed of school and university leavers making itself felt in the workplace.

Born between 1980 and 1995 these young people live and breathe the internet, the iPod, Facebook, gap years and student debt. Variously known as Millennials, Generation Y (Gen Y) or the Net Generation, they are busily intent on rewriting the

[5] Ibid.

rules. Apart from their age, they have in common their demand for a better work–life balance, an impatience for recognition and a readiness to challenge accepted management practice every which way. Putting it slightly differently, they are redefining what constitutes a great place to work and this is inducing a new centre of gravity for those who manage talent.

Not everyone agrees that Gen Y is so different from those who went before them. US and European studies in 2009 into the attitudes of Gen Y suggest that they are not that different from other generations as is supposed, and not just because the recession upset their expectations. While craving excitement and challenge, nearly 90% of Gen Y describe themselves as loyal to their employer.

Gen Y though may be more determined to pursue a work–life balance than has previously eluded the earlier Boomers and Gen X, those in their thirties and forties. For example, a promising young trader with a US investment bank was told he would be promoted if he could complete a gruelling five-month training programme in just three months. Deciding that the personal price was too high he turned the offer down twice before deciding to quit to coach a university soccer team.[6]

In the Maynard Leigh 2009 report, 'Talent Management at the Crossroads', nearly all of the 20 companies surveyed were sympathetic to the needs of Gen Y. Positive comments from HR directors included:

- 'There's a fearlessness and sense of self-confidence among Gen Y.'
- 'They feel empowered to ask the right questions.'
- 'They want and expect more of a work–life balance.'
- 'They have had to do things quicker and better.'[7]

An important implication for managing talent, suggested the report, is the need to abandon a mindset in which frequent job changes equates to a decline in loyalty to an employer. If young people are less prepared to stay with one company, they compensate by loyalty to their career giving talent managers important levers to pull, such as offering training or fast-track career development.

Globalisation

Controversially, globalisation is opening the door for highly talented migrant workers to a burgeoning worldwide market for talent, aided by increasingly harmonised employment laws and qualifications frameworks.

Professional services firms like PwC, McKinsey, and law firms like Lovells and Linklaters, for example, regularly offer their graduate recruits the chance to work in one of their overseas branches on a short-term contract for a year. This provides them with a chance to learn a different business culture and legal context.

[6] Alison Maitland (2009) 'A to Z of Generation Y attitudes', *Financial Times*, 18 June.
[7] Maynard Leigh report (2009) *Management Talent* 'at the Crossroads'.

It tends to be the younger Gen Y professionals who take advantage of these offers. They see it as part of their professional development, an experience that will give them exposure to other parts of the organisation as well as the confidence to handle challenging situations early on.

Work–life balance

The more talented the employee the more likely he or she will need help to ensure a suitable work-life balance. These employees are often driven not by mainly financial rewards, but other factors such as the opportunity to make a difference. In the drive to succeed, such people can easily become job rather mission addicted.

Talent managers need to understand and value the importance of maintaining a work–life balance and should do more than just urge others to achieve it. They need to model a balance in their own lives too.

The work–life balance

Karen Quigley, a senior development engineer at Edwards in Shoreham West Sussex, a manufacturer of vacuum pumps for clean rooms, has negotiated a flexible working arrangement with her employer. She spends more time at home bringing up her young family, a boy and a girl aged 5 and 6, working four days a week spread over five days.

The nature of the work and the supporting technology means that Quigley fits the school run and the children's bedtime around her busy schedule: 'Edwards is a global company and I liaise with my opposite numbers in the States, in Japan and Korea. I tend to work in short, intensive bursts. Because of international time zones I can be on the phone for several hours after the children have gone to bed working on quality issues with engineers on the other side of the world who are installing our pumps.'

Organisational context

The organisation itself is the third context in which talent managers must operate and take into account a variety of factors, including in particular business strategy and employee engagement.

In past millennia the Chinese had a saying: 'The mountains are high and the emperor is far away.' For many of today's managers this is how they view their company's business strategy – distant and not having much immediacy. But making the best use of talent means lifting one's eyes to the mountains and helping people gain a wider vision of what the organisation is trying to achieve.

This context demands more clarity about what talent management means and indeed what is to be defined as 'talent'. As a result of a detailed study, Ashridge reported in 2007 that 'most organisations define "talent" through some reference to potential, in particular high potentials. For other organisations, though, talent was defined as a critical skill set which has become difficult to obtain in the labour market.'[8]

The American Society for Training & Development also found that 'talent can mean different things to different organisations', and that research showed that there is rarely a commonly agreed definition.[9] Studies in the UK too have suggested that few organisations have arrived at a formal definition of talent management.

The provocative issue of inclusiveness versus an exclusive approach must also be confronted and the implications understood for the kind of development investment the company will make.

Similarly, it is not enough to just attract individuals with high potential. Developing and retaining them must become part of a planned approach including finding ways to measure the return on this investment.

In fact, relatively few companies have evolved robust systems for clarifying the benefits from investing in talent. We suggest a growing demand on talent managers will be their ability to demonstrate the benefits from attracting and retaining talent.

The richness and complexity of the organisational context makes it tempting to consider handing over the whole issue of managing talent to HR specialists. However, as the Economist Intelligence Unit reported in 2006,[10] CEOs generally say that 'talent management is too important to be left just to the HR function'.

Within large companies HR will normally play an important role in designing and developing the talent management framework. But the practicalities of identifying and development of talent should still rest with line managers with responsibilities for these precious human resources.

Zurich: linking talent strategy to business objectives

 'We continue to make sure our talent strategy is strongly linked to business objectives,' says HR director Chris McCormack. He explains how Zurich has created a talent management culture with line managers being trained as talent managers.

'We have adapted our talent management strategy to take account of the present economic context. Rather than reducing our focus on our high talent population, we have sought to make efficiencies in our talent management spend,' he concludes.

[8] Ashridge Consulting and Chartered Management Institute (2007) 'Talent Management: Maximising talent for business performance', November.
[9] ASTD Research (2009) 'How Do You Define Talent Management?', 8 May.
[10] Economist Intelligence Unit (2006) 'The CEO's Role in Talent Management: How top executives from ten countries are nurturing the leaders of tomorrow', EIU paper in conjunction with Development Dimensions International (DDI).

Bourne Leisure: matching talent to strategic aims and vision

Q *Matching talent to the strategic aims and vision of the organisation calls for a tailored and often highly flexible approach. Bourne Leisure, the UK holiday camp business, noted the sudden decline in the sterling exchange rate which made foreign holidays more expensive. It spotted a new business opportunity in encouraging people to have more holidays in the UK. So it diverted its training and development budget to up-skill its customer-facing staff such as receptionists, sales and retail managers to promote its products in a more proactive manner.*

PwC

Q *PwC linked talent to strategy by concluding that not attracting talent through a downturn could have serious long-term consequences for its business. Training and development manager Mick Holbrook told us: 'During the recession of the 90s big firms, including our own, experimented with reducing the graduate intake. As a result, when the upturn came management skills were in short supply and we were left with key gaps. We're certainly not making that mistake this time round.'*

Employer's context

The final context in which talent managers operate is the supply of talent. We discuss elsewhere the myth of the war for talent and that talent is in fact abundant. With often high levels of unemployment and the continued under-use of women and ethnic minorities, there remains plenty of scope to recruit people with talent, depending of course on your definition of talent.

While there may be no overall talent shortage, it may still be hard to fill certain roles in organisations, particularly when it comes to finding appropriate new leaders. For line managers, specific skill shortages can prove a headache, undermining the progress of projects and perhaps affecting overall team performance. This is why it pays to give attention to the succession planning process, which helps answer the question: 'Where will I find my next recruit with the skills I need?' The answer should be 'from our available talent pool' but as we have seen, a narrow interpretation of talent can mean that the size of the pool is far too small.

Even when the 'pool' is interpreted in the broadest sense as including all employees, there may still be discontinuities and the art of talent management is often developing ways to deal with these failings. For example, the main skill shortages in the UK identified by the 2007 National Employers Skills Survey11 were technical or practical skills (52%), oral communication skills (33%) and customer handling skills (32%). Appropriate counteraction by employers has included direct investment in developing these abilities.

During a recessionary climate the pool can look deceptively smooth, with plenty of talent on hand and individuals unlikely to make sudden jumps out of it to be employed elsewhere. But as a YouGov survey reported in 2009,[12] while three out of four people were not planning to change their employer in the near future, over a third admitted that ideally they would like to change jobs. Of these, over half said they were considering moving to a different employment sector or changing career completely. The implication is that employee dissatisfaction is building up like water behind a dam, likely to break when labour market conditions improve.

For talent managers this situation represents both an opportunity and a threat. Once job opportunities increase, those who can will vote with their feet. So it is important not to take for granted people's loyalty and continue investing in engagement practices.

As David Fairhurst, HR Chief at McDonald's and voted HR's most influential practitioner puts it:

> It's too easy to stop doing all these things like engagement, creativity and experimentation and go right to the other end and say, now is the time to make sure that people have a desk and you don't bark at them – that's very short sighted.[13]

Key terms

Engagement

A key aspect of talent management is the ability of every manager to engage people in the work to be done. A core part of talent management is about generating high levels of engagement because these can beneficially affect critical parts of a business, including profits, sales, retention rates, safety, greater productivity, higher levels of innovation, lower rates of sickness and absence.

Incidentally, talent management and talent engagement are not interchangeable; the former is broader and encompasses the role of generating engagement.

Employee surveys

Increasingly, companies are moving beyond a simple measurement of employee satisfaction towards identifying and improving drivers that are proving most effective at engaging employees in their jobs, their companies and their work groups. Here employee surveys are an important tool, part of a diagnostic that gives a snapshot of why your people think as they do.

[11] National Employers Skills Survey 2007, Learning and Skills Council.
[12] YouGov/Chartered Quality Institute Salary Survey, 2009.
[13] Employee Engagement podcast MeetTheBossTV training video 2010, www.meettheboss.tv

A report by Best Companies[14] links successful employee engagement to increased levels of productivity by way of self-evaluation and continuous improvement. Companies taking part in this survey benchmark themselves against others in their sector. For them, the benefit stems from being able to gather raw data that may identify which parts of the organisation are underperforming.

Surveys can also be underpinned with focus groups in which staff pinpoint issues with line managers, or where working conditions are holding back productivity. Useful though these methods are, ultimately what matters is that companies do something positive with the resulting information.

Top-down approach

To make an impact, talent management has to become a board commitment, it needs ongoing support from the top of the organisation, but must also be a corporate-wide approach that amounts to a cultural commitment to unlock people's potential.

It is not enough for managers to merely subscribe to the idea of talent management. There must be a responsibility for ensuring that there is a coherent, workable route map for achieving it in practice.

Talent strategy

See above (p. 14).

Growing your own

A common theme running through many talent management strategies is the desire of companies to grow their own talent, rather than having to import it at considerable cost.

With an elitist approach this means identifying the high potentials and nurturing them appropriately. For example, at Bacardi-Martini Ltd the HR director Allison Campbell told us: 'We've identified around 20% of the workforce as rising stars. These are promotable people who we expect executives will spend a lot of time with.' Yet even with such an elitist approach the company uses a rigorous appraisal process to develop its entire staff and help them develop their careers.

In a tough economic climate astute companies have adjusted their strategy to make cutbacks in recruitment, while giving more emphasis to developing the potential of their own employees. Growing your own talent is invariably cheaper and more effective than recruiting it, particularly in mid-career.

---

[14] www.bestcompanies.co.uk.

Succession planning

Without succession planning, talent management becomes something of a contradiction. To successfully manage talent, whether as an elitist or more inclusive approach, requires a clear view of corporate needs both in the short and the long term.

In about 40% of the companies we spoke to, succession provided a sharp focus for talent management. When confronting turbulent times, even those with a non-elitist approach to talent placed succession planning strongly on their radar.

The dual tasks of helping all employees perform at their best and succession planning should not be regarded as mutually exclusive. As ex-Group Head of Talent and Executive Resourcing at Lloyds Banking Group Jacqueline Davies put it, these are 'two sides of the same coin: talent is about individuals, succession planning is about roles'.

Succession planning is also important in helping companies manage business risk. Policy makers need the assurance that there is a logical and planned method for ensuring they have the right talent in the right place when they need it. Formalised succession planning is a complex mix of monitoring recruitment and attrition rates and identifying future skill gaps. Invariably it ends up being a top-down approach in which career development goes hand in hand with remuneration policy. The outcome is, hopefully, a steady supply of vacancies at the right level to stretch candidates.

Ethical dimension

Talent management also poses ethical and moral dilemmas of which practising line managers need to be at least aware. These might include answers to the following questions:

- Must talented high flyers conform to the cultural norms of the organisation?
- Does being identified as 'talent' mean a licence to be authentic, to be an individual.
- How do you deal with people who do not want to be singled out as talented?
- Does corporate social responsibility impinge on talent management practices and if so how?

An unintended result of trying to accelerate people's development paths may be to arrest their moral development. One study, for example, has found that the more work experience a person has the more ethical their behaviour.

Conclusion

Describing talent management is rather like nailing jelly to the wall. Because it is often an intricate undertaking it is difficult to define. In a 2006 CIPD learning and development survey,[15] for example, only one in five respondents even had a formal definition of talent management. And although over half said they undertake talent management activities, on closer inspection there were considerable variations in what they meant by talent and talent management.

As we have seen, one can view talent management through different filters each with slightly different implications for action. For the moment, though, we will use a simple definition of talent management, knowing that it really has many dimensions, facets and layers that determine what it means in practice.

 Briefing lessons

- While accepting that talent management can be a diffuse area to define, it nevertheless offers a specific definition:

    Talent Management is what an organisation does to recruit, retain and develop talent for its future benefit and it is linked closely to strategy, organisational culture and change management.

- A talent management strategy includes certain key areas of an organisation's operation including recruitment, performance management, career development, succession planning and employee engagement processes.
- The demand and supply for talent and talent management as an activity is broadly encompassed within four contexts that managers need to be aware of: external, workforce, organisational and employers. Each has implications for management practice.
- The external context requires talent managers to take into account an increasingly competitive environment within which to consider the best use of talent. It includes ever-changing government policies, technological development and prevailing levels of employment.
- The workforce context is mainly about the supply of talent and includes, for example, demographic forces, diversity, globalisation and the work–life balance. Mastering this context requires talent managers to be open-minded and constantly exploring what factors are affecting the workforce's environment.

[15] CIPD (2006) 'Change Agenda: Reflections on Talent Management', p. 3.

- The organisational context poses many challenges to talent managers including corporate governance, business strategy and employee engagement.
- The employer's context requires talent managers to understand the demand for human resources, including the issues of skill shortages and competition of talent. The so-called war for talent is deemed something of a myth, partly created by those with a vested interest in promoting such a concept.

Why talent management?

3

- Risks, rewards and tomorrow's reality
- Strategy
- Risks
- Costs
- Rewards
- Priorities: tomorrow's reality
- Actions

Risks, rewards and tomorrow's reality

Talent management is a strategic imperative for organisations. Changing demographics, a willingness of a younger generation to move if their organisations do not meet their expectations, a need for organisations to constantly innovate and to be constantly adaptable, all mean that retaining and developing people are critical success factors. According to a CIPD survey carried out in 2010,[1] among companies undertaking talent management activities in the UK about half considered them effective and just 3% very effective. And in an earlier study three out of four respondents reported that their organisation did not have a well-developed plan for talent management.[2]

The reasons you need to spend time pursuing talent management are firstly that this is a route to achieving high levels of performance, secondly it offers companies a hard to emulate competitive advantage and finally it enables the organisation to be highly adaptive, particularly in turbulent times.

Proof that talent management pays off is relatively scarce though hard evidence is accumulating. A study by the Hackett Group in 2009[3] reported both quantitative and qualitative data showing positive operational, financial and performance benefits from talent management. It reported that 'companies with the most mature talent management capabilities achieved the best results in the three performance categories'.

As an activity and an idea, talent management is therefore relevant across the organisational spectrum from private to public sector, from charities and NGOs to the armed forces. For all of them, talent matters and consequently it has become an important and indeed unavoidable job for all managers. While each may possess their own view of what constitutes talent management, it is broadly a series of processes normally within the remit of human resources consisting of: recruitment, performance management, career development, succession planning and employee engagement processes. Some firms have established specific posts relating to leveraging these policies, such as director of talent, or employee engagement director, and so on.

Talent management comprises a cycle of inter-connected activities. If properly conducted these processes will ensure that talent management stays aligned within an organisation. When properly co-ordinated they form a coherent and understandable policy for unlocking people's potential. To some extent talent management is a frame of mind in which the company invests in its people, and helps them develop their potential, their skills and their performance. Investment in talent and realigning the priorities of the company are a way of boosting creativity, productivity and the quality of service.

[1] CIPD (2010) 'Annual Survey Report 2010: Learning and Talent Development', p. 3.
[2] CIPD (2007) 'Talent Management: Understanding the Dimensions'.
[3] The Hackett Group (2009) 'Key findings from Hackett's Performance Study on Talent Management Maturity', October.

According to CIPD research published in 2010[4] almost one in six organisations undertake talent management activities. The number of employers involved in activities such as performance management, tailored career development, coaching, mentoring and evaluation is rapidly increasing, from 36% in 2006 to 59% in 2010. However, this does not mean their organisations had a well-developed plan for talent management. There is usually some form of talent management with different levels of strategic engagement.

While talent management can take a wide variety of meanings, for many organisations it is usually a relatively simple cycle (see Figure 3.1).

Figure 3.1 The talent management cycle

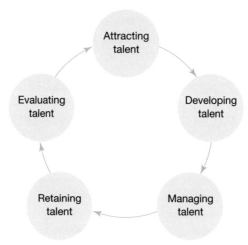

Why bother?

According to research conducted by the CIPD, 60% of organisations have no formal talent management strategy – 50% of respondents undertake talent management activities, although only 20% report having a full definition of it. Even companies with no coherent talent strategy will set people apart in order to raise their potential and performance. This is how they have developed future leaders, and methods can be formal or informal, from a graduate training programme to shadowing the CEO.

Management self-selection can end up working against talent by embedding a command and control culture and an outdated set of values. Organisations are narrowing their options by recruiting the same kinds of people from the same background. By doing so, they fail to plan for a future which will be shaped by dynamic change.

[4] See note 1.
[5] CIPD (2006) 'The Talent Paradox: Learning and Development Survey'.

Talent management is about unlocking people's potential and taking risks along the way. Building a diverse workforce based on fairness and opportunity opens the door to talent. Any organisation that fails to maximise its talent pool is losing its competitiveness. The sad fact is that many employers believe that it's safer to stick with what you know.

Talent management only makes sense when linked directly with the organisation's overall business goals. These goals, or rather their implications for decision making, directly determine the demand for talent.

Strategy

A talent management strategy is essentially a road map for how the organisation will use its people resources for achieving its longer-term goals. To create a strategy requires achieving clarity about defining talent, developing talent and the structures and systems required for promoting talent. For such a map to be really useful a three-year or longer time horizon is recommended.

Talent strategy is rather an abstract concept and easily misunderstood. It makes more sense to specify what you are trying to achieve. For example:

- to develop high potential employees
- to grow future senior leaders
- to secure competitive advantage
- to meet the future skills needs of the organisation
- to reinforce culture and values.

Without a coherent talent management strategy, though, an organisation is undoubtedly missing a trick. As we have seen, talent management is all about unlocking people's potential and using this to help the organisation adapt and grow. An effective talent strategy encourages a disciplined approach to charting how using its people will reach the organisation's longer-term goals.

Francis Mok, Group Human Resources Director of Jebsen & Co and President of the Hong Kong Institute of Human Resource Management, sums it up neatly: 'Putting in place a talent management strategy is critical in an organisation's structure. This is common knowledge in the business world. However, how many companies are actually practising this effectively?'

To Adrian Powell, HR Director of Britannia Building Society, talent management strategy means getting 'the right people now and for key roles in the future'. For example, if your organisation sees an opportunity to build up its overseas network then it will need people with language skills as well as entrepreneurial skills to run standalone operations.

To David Fairhurst, HR Chief at McDonald's, talent management these days is 'all about projecting the operational income of an organisation – where the business is going to make money, what the talent implications and gaps are from that, how things need to evolve and where you are going to get it from.'

To Chris McCormack, Head of the Zurich Academy, UK, talent management strategy is primarily to get best value for money. Talent strategy is decided by the Zurich insurance group's main board in Switzerland and implemented by the various national businesses with regional modifications. The strategy is based on employee surveys and company performance. Faced with a difficult economic climate McCormack explains that 'rather than reducing our focus on our high-talent population, we have sought to make efficiencies in our talent management spend. We continue to make sure our talent strategy is strongly linked to business objectives.'

Without a meaningful talent strategy, selection can become narrow and distorted, or lead to embedding outdated ideas such as a command and control culture, or preserving no longer relevant values. Most organisations have an evolving talent management strategy, rather than one that is fixed and immutable. For example, 'Tata's talent management strategy,' explains Dr Sangram Tambe, VP of Corporate HR, 'focuses on competence, engagement, and growth and development ... but ultimately engaging talent is the most important factor.'

Organisations are often at different stages of strategy development, which may progress in several different directions (see Figure 3.2).

Figure 3.2 Different stages

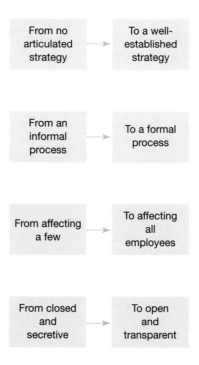

From no articulated strategy	→	To a well-established strategy
From an informal process	→	To a formal process
From affecting a few	→	To affecting all employees
From closed and secretive	→	To open and transparent

Source: adapted from CIPD 'Talent: Strategy Management Measurement', p. 16, 2007.

Risks

Talent management is like a supertanker steaming through an ocean. It is hard to change direction in the short term and long-term trends must be accurately anticipated and prepared for. For example, the recession of the early 90s proved a wake-up call for large consultancy groups: their fairly universal response to the downturn was to cease recruiting. That proved an expensive mistake, and even now some still suffer from yawning skills gaps in key areas. Such consultancies have learned their lessons and in the new millennium downturn many maintained their investment in developing their people and continued to build their skills.

Without an effective talent pipeline, filling an organisation's skill gaps can soon become an issue. Previously, firms could rely on poaching staff from rivals even if it pushed up wage rates in their business sector. This solution to attracting talent is becoming increasingly difficult to rely on for various reasons. So, ultimately, good talent management is about good business planning.

The rapid pace of change, both technological and societal, and the trend towards globalisation has undermined employers' assumptions about talent. Globally, the rise of India and China puts pressure on old economic models. And in 2010 a report called 'Transitions', from BDO and the Centre for Future Studies, issued a stark warning that the UK's business environment 'will never return to pre-recession normality' and that some business models would 'wither away and die'.

A new economic situation based on creative destruction demands that companies do more with less. Talent management will play a key role as employers are forced to make as much use of everyone within the organisation as they demand of the elite few. Increasingly organisations will need to reflect the more diverse nature of society or the markets they serve. They need to cast the net wider for talent.

Finally, in its narrow interpretation, talent management risks antagonising a large number of employees who feel excluded by seeing scarce resources directed towards a select few, labelled 'high potentials'. Focusing limited resources in this way may seem to make perfect sense in tough times; yet in the longer term it may sow the seeds of a culture in which people do not feel valued or fully developed.

Small companies

Small businesses, particularly those where the entrepreneur is in charge of the day to day running of the firm, can be extremely cynical about talent management, regarding it as yet another layer of bureaucracy, like the dreaded 'health and safety' – something that must be complied with. But the theories and practice of talent management apply whether your business has five, 50 or 500 employees. There is always scope for talent management whatever the size and nature of the business, whether it is a small manufacturer, a retailer, a professional consultancy or a partnership.

Nor should the lack of a dedicated human resources department prevent you from adopting a workable talent management policy. For example, Henry Stewart, Chief Executive of Happy, a small computer training company argues: 'The key to a happy workplace is involving as many people in developing the key skills needed to run the business.'

Costs

Investing in talent management is expensive. But the price for treating talent management as a purely optional investment will prove more costly in the long run.

In fact, the business case for investing in talent management appears to be a no-brainer. There is now a wide appreciation of the benefits in terms of creating the next generation of leaders, boosting productivity and filling potential skill gaps. There has been a rapid growth in talent management activities even in a period of economic difficulty with nearly three in five organisations now undertaking such activities. The focus of these activities is mainly on developing high potentials and growing future leaders, linked to creating transformational leaders who have a strong impact on individual, team and organisational performance.

Why invest in talent?

'Commercial priorities and investment in people is not an "either/or". We recognise that what our leaders do shapes the culture,' says Adrian Powell of Britannia Building Society. 'Our investment in leadership and talent will take us forward in terms of where we need to be.'

Despite the fact that talent management makes sense, few employers willingly sign a blank cheque for recruiting and retaining the best. All the HR directors we interviewed linked their talent management strategies with business priorities suggesting that generally business drives talent management and not the other way around.

In being able to make a case for talent management, it is important to develop meaningful metrics and set up benchmarks that can show the gains from doing so. For example, to win boardroom support, often HR must show the business case for investing in people. This means proving the return on investment from training or demonstrating where the talent priorities should lie, and whether these should alter. For example, one talent director of a FTSE 100 company told us: 'The recession has helped us prioritise. We now run one grad scheme where in the past we ran three. We now get more bang for our bucks.'

Similarly, when Mott MacDonald introduced its new professional development programme to boost engineers' commercial skills in civil engineering, it had to ration availability. In a recessionary climate this structured training was clearly regarded as a privilege not an entitlement. 'We didn't have resources to develop everyone as that would mean a programme of 800 a year,' says Group Learning and Development Manager, Carole Teacher. 'People must show they will benefit from the programme and demonstrate they are motivated. We're trying to help people move their careers on inside the company rather than outside.'

And finally a one size fits all approach to talent management appears to be going out of fashion. Companies are instead adopting a more tailor-made approach, directing spending towards interventions that can make the most impact.

Engineering consultancy Atkins, for example, engages with its people as individuals, having developed what its Director of Training and Development, Brian FitzGerald, describes as 'a more holistic approach to talent'. The recession has made Atkins 'focus more on deploying talent effectively and on redeploying talent within the company. Individuals don't have to aspire solely to becoming a business manager in order to do well. We have three career routes to ensure individuals are valued equally if they have technical, business or project management expertise … You can have a career, not just a job in Atkins.'

The Atkins approach highlights the issue of whether talent will be treated as restricted to a few high potentials or, as in Atkins, there may be many ways for talent to be rewarded and developed. However, CIPD evidence suggests that in the UK two out of three organisations view talent management as being concerned with developing high potential employees and to grow future senior managers and leaders.

Rewards

While there are clearly risks associated with talent management there are also many positive rewards which managers and leaders need to consider. Perhaps the most notable reward is that talent management helps ground business goals in the reality of having the right people at the right time in the right roles. There is little point, for example, in having ambitious plans for the future if there is no suitable leadership in place to pursue them.

For example, what type of skills will the organisation need if it is to meet its short- and long-term objectives? Effective talent management can help answer this question with evidence that can guide decision making about how best to develop the available talent. In a 2010 CIPD study,[6] for instance, the CIPD identified the likely necessary skills as:

- leadership skills
- front line people management skills
- business skills
- communication skills.

[6] CIPD (2010) 'Annual Survey Report 2010: Learning and Talent Development'.

A second reward from adopting talent management is it the ability to provide a common language for making decisions about investing in people. As Thomas DuFore, VP of Human Resources for the Henkel Corporation in Germany explains: 'through our talent management tools we are improving our language across the organisation in terms of who our potentials are.'

Succession planning, for example, can be put on a more systematic and transparent basis, and individual careers can be mapped out for the benefit of both individuals and the organisation. Succession, for example, is something that Tesco is known to get right. If Sir Terry Leahy's announcement in 2010 that he'd be retiring the following year in March came as a surprise, the smoothness of the handover to IT and International Director Phil Clarke didn't. Leahy's own appointment as CEO was perfectly executed by the then Tesco boss Lord MacLaurin, credited with taking Tesco from a 'pile 'em high, sell 'em cheap' purveyor of basics to the 'darling of the sundried tomato classes'.

A third reward from talent management is that it helps reduce attrition rates. People who feel their talent is recognised and valued are generally more willing to stay and help make a difference, rather than leaving for greener pastures. A fourth reward from talent management practices is that it allows the organisation to take advantage of new opportunities. By investing in people and developing their capabilities organisations make themselves more ready for handling change. Finally, talent management helps make best use of the limited resources for investing in people's development.

In addition, by systematically pursuing talent management within an organisation talent is more likely to be shared out fairly. For example, departments that attract more than their fair share of talent may find it is lured away by less successful parts of the organisation. With a proper talent management approach agreements can be devised so that talent is neither hoarded nor allowed to be moved prematurely.

However, the ultimate reward from talent management is that it produces people willing to go the extra mile. They do so because of their engagement and willingness to offer discretionary effort. Talent management is a way of systematically drawing forth that effort.

Leveraging the talent within

To justify the investment in talent management there is one reality that even hardened sceptics find difficult to ignore. This is the powerful and universal human desire to grow and develop. It finds expression in the work setting in various ways, many of which demand attention from those in charge. This urge is a virtually unstoppable force, as individuals seek ingenious ways to expand their capabilities and fulfil their potential, with or without the active support of their seniors.

Many leaders and managers embrace the idea of encouraging human development: they see its inevitability and welcome the ideal of an employee who demands to grow and use their potential. Such employees are often regarded favourably as the ones most likely to assist with new ideas and support continuous improvement. At the other end of the spectrum there are many organisations that rely on employing people, sometimes large numbers of them, for whom personal growth at work is not a priority or even of particular interest. However, a diminishing proportion of organisations can afford to function in this way. They pay a high price in lost performance, and in the absence of a stream of new ideas or insights about how to improve products or services.

Talent management must aim to ensure that people have meaningful work in which they can feel fully engaged and hence willing to go that extra mile. Certainly amongst developed economies there is less and less scope to rely on people doing brain-numbing routine.

Nurturing talent throughout your organisation is not so much a luxury as a sound approach to drawing on a wide spectrum of talent. Astute leaders realise that new ideas do not just come from the high potentials in their organisation and recognise the importance of being receptive to innovation from all levels of the enterprise. This is why Google's famous 20% allowance for its engineers to spend time on whatever they choose is so effective. It ensures a constant stream of creative ideas of how to grow the business. Similarly, Marks & Spencer's talent management strategy includes a clear commitment to encourage innovation at all levels. By including this statement among its core values, the company aims to differentiate itself in the marketplace and gain competitive advantage.

Midlands metal-bashing company BEC Engineering has used the talent of its workers to invent a new product to boost sales in a declining market. The Warwickshire company staff worked together to solve the problem of low order books by designing and constructing high-quality stainless steel planters for garden centres and offices. 'We realised we had to expand our core business and reach new customers,' says the company's Managing Director Duncan Barnsley. Giving staff the freedom to develop new lines, based on their hands-on knowledge and understanding of what their customers needed, is expected to yield a higher profit margin and add 20% to turnover.

Finally, leveraging talent or making the best use of what you have got can also help with diversity. While for some leaders talent management mainly means succession planning targeted at an elite, for others it is sufficiently inclusive to absorb diversity as well. Putting it slightly differently, if you want to make meritocracy really work you will need to consider the implications for promoting diversity.

Of those organisations that undertake talent management activities, four out of five integrate diversity and equality considerations in their talent management process, at least to some extent. In contrast, about a fifth do not integrate diversity or know whether they do.

Contributing to growth

No matter what your industry, company or nationality there is a battle-ready competitor somewhere who is busy thinking how to beat you. While products can be rapidly duplicated and services cheaply emulated, innovation, execution and knowledge cannot. So the collective talent of an organisation is its prime source in competing and winning. In the kind of environment in which your organisation may have to operate and seek to grow, the new competitive advantage is smart, committed, experienced people who are technologically literate, globally astute and operationally agile.

Even as you seek growth, talent management is likely to top the list as a way of radically improving workforce performance and to drive higher value for the organisation. Without effective talent management, the organisation's survival, let alone growth, may simply prove illusionary. It is also important to recognise that talent management is an integrated way of contributing to growth, rather than relying on functional silos. If it is to make a difference the various processes must be properly integrated into the organisation's way of doing things – that is it must fundamentally affect its culture. When that occurs expected benefits include:

- rapid product introductions
- improved sales delivery
- increased innovation
- lower production costs
- increased on-time and on-budget projects
- higher customer satisfaction
- sustained organisational improvements.

Priorities: tomorrow's reality

While talent management is increasingly in vogue, it will eventually cease to dominate developmental thinking and activities. As Francis Mok, Group HR Director of Jebsen & Co, the marketing and distribution organisation for premium products in Greater China and beyond puts it:

> Talent management will not offer any competitive advantage 10 years from now, as those who pay no attention to talent management will already be extinct from the market. The earlier one takes on proper planning and implements talent management the more one's chance of survival increases.

As we have noted, there is no best or one way to 'do' talent management. Each organisation needs to align its talent management system to its own business goals. This is the secret of successful talent management and ensures its total relevance to both line managers and policy makers. To really flourish talent management needs more than just a managerial or leadership commitment, welcome though that may be. It requires to be totally embedded in the organisation's culture so that talent conversations become the norm.

In developing talent management for the 21st century it is also necessary to make certain assumptions about the likely shape of the future workforce. Already the outline seems clear. Given continuing trends to outsource both services and production to the best location, the future workforce available to many companies is likely to be global, diverse and gender balanced.

In managing talent, managers also need to be comfortable with the clear trend towards discontinuous career progressions. Instead of total loyalty to the organisation it means accepting that talented employees may take time off or work for different types of organisations along the way. Similarly, for new generations of employees in an ever faster-moving digital age, non-monetary rewards look likely to play a greater part in attracting and retaining talent. Issues such as a balanced life style, making the organisation socially responsible, environmentalism and ethical considerations look set to play a far greater part in influencing where talented young people want to work. These in turn seem set to fundamentally affect how companies both develop their talent and whether they can successfully retain it to avoid lethal levels of attrition.

Actions

Actions you can take right now to become more talent friendly include:

- learning how well your organisation knows the demographic characteristics of its workforce
- discovering what your organisation knows about the attitude of employees
- learning how competitors leverage talent
- checking how alert your top team is to the integral nature of talent management and promoting diversity
- ensuring talent management practices within your control specifically encourage innovation
- mastering the essentials of what creates high levels of employee engagement.

Remember: if you want to grow the organisation, be sure to grow your people.

Briefing lessons

- Globally, the rise of India and China puts pressure on old economic models. Talent management can help secure higher levels of employee engagement, boosting business performance and profitability. It offers companies competitive advantage and enables organisations to be highly adaptive, particularly in turbulent times.
- Retaining and developing people are critical success factors for any business or organisation. Employers need to be aware of changing demographics in the workforce and develop a talent strategy that will appeal equally to men and women from a wide range of backgrounds and across a wide age range. Greater willingness among younger employees to change jobs if their working conditions or job satisfaction falls short of expectations means organisations are having to develop innovative forms of employee engagement.
- To really flourish, talent management needs to be more than just an add-on. It must be totally embedded in the organisation's culture so that talent conversations become the norm.
- Good talent management is about aligning HR strategy to business planning. Without an effective talent pipeline, skill gaps can quickly become an issue. Leadership competencies align the aims of the company or organisation with the individual. Effective succession planning can enable the organisation to grow its next generation of leaders.

Who's doing it?

4

Introduction

Talent management is a process. No two companies will adopt it in exactly the same way; each is on a separate and unique journey towards making the best use of talent. It is important to develop a vision for talent management as process. For example, one company may see it as mainly about building a high-performance workplace, while another may interpret it as encouraging a learning organisation.

The art of talent management is to adapt your style and approach to respond to your particular local conditions and context. As a talent manager your starting point is recognising that people have different capabilities and respecting this by treating each employee as an individual.

What makes talent management so compelling? It is when managers like you actively set out to link it directly with business priorities. This involves learning what it will take to foster improved performance which will have an impact on bottom-line profits.

Today, talent management is increasingly recognised by companies not merely as desirable, but as a commercial imperative. But it is hard to define as a single unambiguous concept. Instead, you will find it easier to view it, as it were, through different coloured filters:[1]

- process
- cultural necessity
- competitive drive
- developmental approach
- HR activity.

In recent years, these have crystallised into the fundamentals of talent management that no ambitious and thoughtful manager can afford to ignore.

In essence, talent management is a broad-brush approach to managing people, starting with strategy, but evolving into practical steps for realising the strategy. It is not like a fancy sports car that we take for a spin and then return to the garage. Instead, it is about ways in which an organisation marshals all its policies and resources to achieve a single aim: maximising the use of talent to achieve its business goals. This includes all aspects of talent management such as recruitment, retention, succession planning and gaining commitment to aim for outstanding performance.

---

[1] Blass, Dr Eddie (2007) 'Talent Management: Maximising Talent for Business Performance', Executive Summary, Ashridge CCMI, November.

Process

This filter assumes that your company will use all necessary processes to make the best use of available talent. It demands good succession planning and a regular review process so that people are constantly developed, and in some cases have their own personal development plan.

It is important also to be aware that whatever process you choose may well affect practices throughout your organisation, for example with respect to recruitment and selection, retention, succession planning and the development approach that your organisation adopts.

Using this filter means, for instance, being focused on personal development plans as part of performance management. In the case study below, RBS has been able to motivate its staff to take charge of their own career development, helping them to see that they are contributing directly to the company's growth plans.

RBS: an inclusive approach to talent management

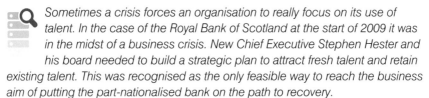

Sometimes a crisis forces an organisation to really focus on its use of talent. In the case of the Royal Bank of Scotland at the start of 2009 it was in the midst of a business crisis. New Chief Executive Stephen Hester and his board needed to build a strategic plan to attract fresh talent and retain existing talent. This was recognised as the only feasible way to reach the business aim of putting the part-nationalised bank on the path to recovery.

The new business priorities were to focus on customers, improve efficiency and reduce risk. Talent management's contribution was to adapt the bank's culture to one where leaders would become developers and enablers of talent.

Where previously top-down policies focused solely on delivering business results, the bank's new priority was for leaders to deliver sustainable results by getting the best out of all people.

'Everyone at RBS has talent,' says Human Resources Director of group organisational effectiveness Janey Smith. She adds: 'Talent means people taking responsibility for developing themselves and fulfilling their potential and we aid this through an internal careers website. We also have processes to identify and facilitate the progress of high potentials and people whose skills we are trying to grow and develop.'

In the midst of a massive restructuring it was critical that leaders were able to set out a clear vision and inspire trust in their people. With risk management now high on the agenda Hester's view was that RBS could only recover if business leaders were open and transparent – even when there was bad news.

One of the key changes at RBS was to align performance management with talent management. Smith explains: 'We have adopted 360-degree feedback as a means of performance assessment. Everyone is assessed in relation to how well they are creating a culture of transparency and responsible risk management in their business and of listening and responding to customers' needs.'

The restructuring is providing ample opportunities for stretching goals and staff development, and front line staff are highly regarded. 'People are telling us that challenge in their job or making a transition to a new role is better development than any amount of classroom training,' says Smith.

With feedback from over 20,000 respondents now providing valuable insight, the bank has launched a leadership development programme to focus on value creation and strategic risk management. Leaders stress test their business plans and develop options for a range of scenarios for everything from changes in the economy to responding to competitor activity.

A new pattern of leadership is emerging and RBS is seeing a shift towards leaders as developers and coaches who enable people to get things done. There is now a stronger emphasis on creative thinking and on being open to new ideas.

Cultural necessity

A second filter influencing talent-oriented companies is having a mindset that talent is regarded as essential for success. Many organisations, though, have yet to make this leap of faith. Those using this filter through which to view talent are likely to recognise that the organisation needs to be constantly on the lookout for raw talent, including drawing in external contacts. It also means allowing people to demonstrate, explore and develop their talent as part of their normal work. One implication is that it will involve negotiating with individuals to create their own development paths and offer support in the form of coaching and mentoring.

Creativity is part of a new culture of change at retailer Marks & Spencer.

Marks & Spencer: maintaining a strong business focus in a competitive market.

Training and development is one of the first things to go in a recession. 'We have increased development. Because it struck me that a number of companies weren't doing any development because of the recession,' says Tanith Dodge, M&S Human Resources Director. She adds, 'What we are doing is in line with our business needs.'

In 2009, M&S recruited 200 graduates to its fast-track graduate induction programme. At the same time it launched new mid-career development programmes, Manage to Succeed, a course in the fundamentals of store management, and Lead to Succeed, a top-level leadership development programme for the retailer's top 100 managers. Training is part of a systematic people-focused agenda that is aligned to business strategy and to the core values of the organisation.

No one is missed out. 'We have programmes for every level,' says Dodge. 'There are programmes that take people through to become a section manager, section manager to store manager, and store manager to regional manager.

We give everyone a development opportunity.' Training and development gives staff the edge and challenge.

By making demands of staff and providing them with stretching goals or development challenges, training reinforces employee engagement. It is a case of tough love according to Dodge: 'There are no jobs for life. And I don't see complacency when I'm out and about in stores.' But as with any comprehensive development programme there are risks. Dodge continues: 'The risk is that if you're not managing talent the best people will move on.' Currently staff turnover at M&S is one of the lowest in the industry at 23%.

Lead to Succeed is a values-focused preparation for the most senior and board level vacancies. Dodge comments: 'Leadership is about using your head and your heart in equal measure – using logic and reason but trusting in gut instinct and your own beliefs.' Lead to Succeed reinforces the M&S core values – trust, value, service, quality and innovation – but it is the last quality that receives the most emphasis.

Innovation or creativity is where M&S aims to compete with its retail rivals. Dodge explains: 'M&S has been around for the past 125 years and people often think we are set in our ways. But we were the first retailer to offer frozen foods and we were first in the field with suits that you can put in the washing machine. Lead to Succeed encourages managers to reflect on their practice and to look for ways of doing things differently.'

One example of leadership development in practice is M&S's head of technology who has worked with manufacturers in India to develop new checks and processes to improve the quality of items such as trainers, blouses and skirts. Another example thrown up by Lead to Succeed was the discovery that different parts of the M&S business based in different locations were doing things quite differently. Dodge says: 'The buyer for our women's collection Limited was based in London while our other fashion brand, Per Una, was based in the Cotswolds and had its own approach. Those two brands are now leveraging and learning from each other.'

Lead to Succeed closes with a feedback session at which managers present their ideas to the Chief Executive and his board. Dodge says: 'They can see that we're providing a return on investment. It gives real live examples of aspiring leaders who are going about doing something differently.'

M&S operates a bonus system to incentivise senior managers. The scheme is based on a mixture of individual and business performance targets. Dodge says: 'Most companies have an individual performance-related incentive scheme. Otherwise why make an effort? If you are outstanding and go the extra mile you expect to engage your people. John Lewis do a profit share and it works for them.'

Competitive drive

This filter is one where you view the organisation's talent as scarce and make sure it is kept well away from the competition. With this approach there is a strong emphasis on retaining talent, on being ready to poach the best from competition and letting people know exactly what they are supposed to achieve.

When seeing talent management in a competitive way one implication is that the organisation needs to become an employer of choice. Supporting this may be planned or opportunistic approaches to developing each person, including providing mentors.

Talent management policies have adapted to changing circumstances as the international consultancy PricewaterhouseCoopers demonstrated when the recession first began to bite. Instead of a freeze on recruitment the firm simply changed tack and started to reassess talent with greater emphasis on role flexibility.

PricewaterhouseCoopers: a university for talent

 Talent management is top of the agenda at PwC and the firm has taken a bullish approach to talent in the downturn. In 2009 this £2 billion revenue business recruited 1,000 graduates in the UK for a variety of roles. Mick Holbrook, Head of Organisation and People Development says: 'The real value to our clients is the high calibre of our people.'

The megamerger between Price Waterhouse and Coopers and Lybrand in 1998 established PwC as the leader not just in professional services but in the quality of its graduate talent programme. Holbrook says, 'Our training supplies not just our own talent needs but to the wider industry. We are supplying CFOs to companies as well as talent to the financial regulators. We feel that we are a university for talent.'

PwC's board has formulated a strategy to deliver a talent management vision that is aligned to business strategy in the short to medium term. It has developed an emerging leader programme in which talent is identified and fast tracked through a CPD partnership with London Business School. For the past five years PwC has topped The Times top 100 graduate employers list, and has consistently made it to the top of the Sunday Times Best 100 Company rankings.

The downturn has put the spotlight on business restructuring, insolvency and business recovery and PwC has responded by moving talent from traditional tax and audit roles to meet these new opportunities.

Developmental activity

Using this filter talent management is geared towards accelerating the growth of high potentials. Here the approach identifies groups of people who will be developed for each level of the organisation. Development is about filling key roles and is a narrow rather than inclusive approach to talent.

This is also likely to involve a strong emphasis on retention of talent, for example by offering clear development paths and schemes to lock high potentials into career paths. International law firm Lovells has a quite specific view of talent as a route to partnership.

Lovells: sourcing senior managers

Operating in highly competitive global markets lawyers need strong commercial skills, enterprise and creativity.

International law firm Lovells has recently appointed a senior partner to represent talent management on the firm's international management board. The move has strengthened the firm's overall HR strategy, reinforcing a more merit-based approach to talent management based on individual appraisal and meaningful conversations regarding careers.

A standardised approach to talent management owned by the board facilitates a common approach to career development across the organisation. This approach represents a move away from the time-honoured practice common among law firms of promotion solely based on years of seniority.

Kay Willis, HR Director, says: 'We're interested in assessing the contribution of senior associates using a merit-based approach. We can benchmark performance based on appraisal and against the competencies expected at each level. It's a qualitative process. HR is currently working on a set of metrics for talent management that the executive Board can agree to. These are likely to include factors like regularity of appraisals, and access to appropriate training.'

Putting process around talent management provides structured experience, additional resources for CPD and a smoother career progression. Willis says: 'There was a real gap between the role performed by partners with their great gamut of responsibility and the role performed by senior associates in the run up to promotion to partner. We've eased that transition.'

HR activity

This filter involves making sure the organisation has the right people in the right jobs at the right time. It can only happen when groups of people at each level of the organisation are identified as needing development. The HR emphasis of this filter means having a detailed approach to mapping career paths, tracking staff turnover and adopting numbers and quotas for target areas of the business.

Meeting the skills needs of the organisation, spirits company Bacardi-Martini has found development opportunities for talent even in recession. Talent management is all about matching business needs and business imperatives with talent strategy.

Bacardi-Martini: talent supports restructuring

Just before the recession really got going, Bacardi-Martini Ltd, the premium spirits company, underwent a major restructuring of its UK business ahead of the recession. The closure of a production and distribution depot in Southampton with the loss of around 250 jobs and the concentration of the commercial business in the Winchester site has put the company in a sound state to weather the downturn.

The company's HR department has a clearly defined talent management strategy with a strong emphasis on succession planning. The company devotes resources to training managers to identify the rising stars and develop them appropriately. This translates into providing them with opportunities for sideways moves as well as promotion.

The company's HR Director Allison Campbell explains: 'It's all about making the connection between personal growth and corporate good. Talent management is a key part of the process of helping people understand where they fit and where they contribute. We go through the talent management process on a six-monthly basis. This is distinct from performance management – how you're doing in your job. Talent management is focused on potential. Do people have the potential to progress?'

The recession has prompted a review of internal mobility and people are now expected to stay longer in their jobs to encourage the development of true expertise. A spin off from this has been people have gained a greater depth of experience and become more committed to continuous professional development.

Campbell says: 'The economic downturn, amongst other things, has prompted us to think about the best way to provide opportunities to move people to different functions and give them different skills. Now it's more important to have strong experience in the role. People stay longer in their roles and become truly proficient. This differentiates us from the competition. A junior manager will stay in post a minimum of two years and a senior manager a minimum of 2–5 years.' Her colleague, HR Manager Claire Palmer, agrees: 'The feedback we've received has been very productive. People are recognising that staying longer is going to be beneficial to their careers. The more we can achieve a true balance of developing depth of skills in roles and providing opportunities for individuals to develop in an appropriate timeframe, the more our business and our people will benefit.'

What do success and failure look like?

Issues of inclusiveness versus an exclusive approach must also be explored and finally resolved. It is not enough to just attract individuals with high poten-tial, developing and retaining them must become part of a planned approach including finding ways to measure the return on this investment. Relatively few companies have evolved robust systems for clarifying the benefits from investing in talent.

Inclusiveness versus a focus on a few highly talented and prized individuals has become a critical issue for many companies. Faced with pressure on overheads and the need to economise, what better than to launch an attack on so-called low performers? This became an act of faith in GE where kicking out the so-called bottom performing 5% of employees every year was regarded as sound talent management. The famous 'rank or yank' approach in which you get promoted or get out, pioneered by the ubiquitous McKinsey organisation along with its invention of the war for talent, has had a disproportionate and some might say adverse influence on managerial behaviour.

If you have any doubts about the merits of adopting an elitist view of talent consider the Enron story. Here was a company that converted the urge for stellar performers into an entire culture. Continuous streams of advanced degree recipients poured into the company through its annual 'feed the talent' recruitment programme. Despite the torrent of talent the company imploded.

So what does all this tell us about inclusive versus exclusive talent?

● First, managers who rely on picking top talent and developing it at the expense of the rest may find they pay a heavy price in terms of loss of engagement, loss of stakeholder support and ultimately in bottom-line performance.

● Secondly, while companies can certainly benefit from employing exceptionally talented people it is the latter's ability to work within an ensemble that probably makes as much or more difference than their singular star quality.

● Thirdly, you are more likely to extract a better financial and business return from an inclusive approach in which talent is seen as residing everywhere.

As can be seen from the case study below, Marriott Hotels has developed a system of talent management that unlocks the potential of all of its staff or 'associates' as it prefers to call them.

Marriott Hotels: walking the talk

Putting its people first is a clear mission statement that has enabled Marriott Hotels to outperform its rivals. The policy of walking the talk is ingrained and for Marriott talent management is about encouraging everyone in the company to maximise their full potential.

Gary Dodds, Regional Vice President HR for the UK, Ireland, Middle East and Africa explains: 'The key for me is the culture. Talent management says something about the organisation – who we are and what we do. When Bill Marriott handed over the reins to his son Bill Junior, his advice was "Forget about targets … put your people first. If you truly get to know your employees and treat them with dignity and respect, then this respect will be reflected in the way they treat your guests. Being made to feel special is what brings guests back and repeat business and customer satisfaction drives profit and turnover and return on investment to turnover too."'

As a management company the chain, which operates as a hotel management company and franchiser, achieves a consistent approach to HR and people processes through communication and employee engagement. Marriott invests a significant amount of its talent management budget in its corporate intranet, a user-friendly site which keeps staff up to date on all aspects of the company, its performance, policies and opportunities. This includes a recruitment website with internal and external vacancies and a candidate management system which receives 450,000 hits a month across the UK, Ireland, Middle East and Africa region. The intranet also features information on discipline issues and other information.

As a response to the downturn Marriott has put a temporary freeze on recruiting, and has implemented a voluntary four-day week across the UK and Ireland. This will help to retain employees, ensure the business survives these very difficult times and emerges from them with its talent intact.

Marriott is continuing to leverage its talent spend by putting an emphasis on retention, engaging with its workforce and on continuing to develop talent from within. Gary Dodds says: 'We want to make sure we do the best for our people even in these difficult times, though, sadly, some redundancies have had to be made. We have invested time and money in creating employee brand awareness. That is the look of the hotel and the advertising that you see when you click on our website as a customer or as an employee. It's a visual brand. We keep investing in our brand even during an employment freeze.'

When Marriott Hotels started comparing staff satisfaction surveys with occupancy rates and profitability it made an interesting discovery. Dodds says: 'When Steven Marriott (Bill's son) decided to analyse the associate satisfaction surveys going back over some years he saw that when the scores were down the business was also down, as was customer satisfaction. But when satisfaction levels were high so too were repeat business and profit.'

'Marriott's leadership culture and philosophy of doing the best for its people even in these hard times is what makes Marriott different,' Dodds added.

In recognising the link between employee engagement, customer satisfaction and bottom-line profitability, Marriott was among the first in the field to recognise the tangible benefits of talent management. It did not arrive at this happy position by being able to pick and choose talented people to recruit but rather it has grown its own talent through carefully tailored development plans and by a company policy geared totally towards rewarding staff who go the extra mile.

Briefing lessons

- Talent management is increasingly recognised by companies as not merely desirable but a commercial imperative. With no easy way of defining it unambiguously each company must arrive at its own view of what it means.
- Given the lack of a universal view of talent management it is useful to view it through five basic filters – process, cultural necessity, competitive drive, developmental approach and HR activity. Each gives a different perspective and is not necessarily mutually exclusive. They merely focus attention on different aspects of how to approach the task of talent management.
- Talent management is a broad-brush approach to managing people, starting with strategy but solidly based on practical steps for bringing it to fruition.
- Companies that take talent management seriously arrive at their own clear picture of what success and failure looks like. For example, one important issue to resolve is whether to adopt an inclusive approach to talent, or a more focused one directed at those viewed as having high potential.
- While there are arguments on both sides for an inclusive approach versus an elitist approach, companies that adopt the latter are likely to lose out in terms of both innovation and loss of engagement amongst those not chosen as high potentials.

[PART TWO]

In practice

How to do it: a step-by-step guide

5

Introduction

Powerful forces are trying to eat away at your organisation, from the inside and out.

From outside, competitors almost certainly want to lure away your top employees, maybe even an entire team, with promises of bigger salaries, fancier perks, more exciting work. Without counteraction their hunger for talent could negate all of your investment and years of effort in building a fine, perhaps world-class organisation. 'As success makes us more visible, head hunters are going to start thinking about our talent,' admits Jackie Lanham, Director of Resourcing and Development at the Co-operative Group. The Group developed its first talent programme to identify future leaders and protect it from losing key staff.

Also from outside, your customers will be ever more demanding. They want better and faster service, or improved and more effective products. For most of them, 'satisfactory' is simply not good enough. To give them what they want and deliver something beyond mere competence will require you to fully use talent within the organisation and beyond.

From the inside, unless your people feel fully engaged and committed there is little chance they will make your customers happy. This is why mastering the talent management role is so important. It also helps counter a host of damaging potential negatives, from fragile profits to avoidable accidents at work.

While your present role may not actually say 'talent manager' in the title, this is surely what you are! Even if you do not see it that way, those above you and others below almost certainly will. Having a clear focus on talent management can turn it from an abstract idea into something highly practical. Areas of focus are ones where being proactive with talent will make a real difference to your organisation. At its simplest, the key steps to making talent management a reality are as shown in Figure 5.1.

Battle hardened managers will recognise how easy it is to become enmeshed in the complexities, many of which are created by HR specialists and in groups drawn from across the organisation. Instead, we suggest that the imperative is to focus on these key elements that make talent management viable:

- be a magnet for talent (recruit)
- cultivate talent (nurture)
- hang onto your talent (retain)
- deal with people trends (demographics).

Figure 5.1 Key steps to making talent management a reality

Define	• what you and your organisation mean by talent management • to whom it will apply, the few or the many
Clarify	• goals driving the organisation • what demands the goals make for specific skills and talents (e.g. leaders)
Identify	• existing pool of talents and skills • how the pool relates to present and future needs
Design	• a talent strategy that fits the organisation, culture and business strategy • ways to challenge assumptions that may be distorting thinking about talent
Develop	• practical actions for recruitment, development and retention of talent • process to ensure all stakeholders are fully informed and stay involved
Implement	• changes on a planned basis • new systems, procedures and monitoring
Evaluate	• whether the organisation has the right skills available when it needs them • ways to adjust talent, based on evidence of its success

Recruit

Like premier league football teams, top companies stand out from the crowd. As employers of choice, they can attract the star players, invest the most in developing them and capture the highest market share. They usually win most of the awards for good people practices too!

If it only took the juiciest financial carrot to lure the talent you need, the whole process of talent management would be easy – throw money at it. While paying high salaries may swamp you with applicants, it still may not attract the necessary talent. Take Generation Y, for example, those born between 1980 and 1995. They tend to take a short-term view of employment. Financial carrots may gain their attention, yet take second place to a demand for varied work experience which boosts their CV and helps build a career.

In fact, the talent you want may be viewing you and your organisation through an entirely different pair of spectacles to those on which you rely. For instance, in the *Sunday Times* 2010 survey of the best small companies to work for, employees were attracted not to those who paid best, but to ones that actively engaged with charities, the environment and their communities.

For people with high potential, lack of career development, inadequate training and an absence of challenging work may all prove to be deal breakers. High potentials, in particular, search for an environment where people like them will be trusted by people like you. They want to be in a place where high standards prevail and to which they can aspire. They are also keen to be somewhere that welcomes their opinions and ideas. Is it like that in your organisation?

Think of recruiting talent as being like operating a magnet. You need to create the right degree of magnetism with:

● the organisation's brand
● effective people practices.

Your brand

Apart from how people view your organisation's products or services, its brand also depends on its reputation as an employer. High potentials naturally gravitate towards those brands where there is a good fit between the explicit values of the organisation and their own values and beliefs. Brand is therefore an important magnet for attracting talent and in conveying that the organisation is 'a good place to work for'. With nationally published reports on such companies, you can be sure that the brightest talent you want is right now scanning the latest list. What will it take to get your company's name on it?

'A good company to work for' is not as nebulous as it seems. It includes measurable factors such as size, reputation and values backed by management practices, all of which shape people's perception of the organisation. Part of being a successful talent manager, therefore, means taking an active interest in the brand. This means discovering, for example, whether it currently helps or hinders in attracting talent. For instance, is there a close alignment between the brand your organisation communicates to potential talent and the reality inside the enterprise?

The smartest employers resist the temptation to present their organisation as more exciting, glamorous or packed with hidden opportunities than the reality justifies. Instead, they delegate their most recent recruits to talk directly to those with potential, sharing honestly what it is like actually working for the organisation.

 Tip

Present your organisation's culture as it really is, rather than some idealised projection that will ultimately cause high attrition rates and damage the brand.

Effective people practices

Your organisation's people practices (see Figure 5.2) will also affect the quality of applicants and therefore influence whether your company becomes a magnet for talent.

Figure 5.2 Your organisation's people practices

Significantly, strong uniformity exists in what people see as key attraction drivers across countries. In a 2006 Towers Perrin study[1] the top attractions in rank order were:

1 competitive base pay
2 work–life balance
3 challenging work
4 career advancement opportunities
5 salary linked to individual performance.

The most effective people practice of all that soon communicates to those thinking of joining is that people in the organisation feel fully engaged with the work. People will be engaged if they feel valued, involved, developed and inspired.

[1] O'Neal, S. and Gebauer, J. (2006) 'Talent management in the 21st century: Attracting, retaining and engaging employees of choice', *World at Work*, Towers Perrin.

Effective management

The general reputation of an organisation's management can strengthen the magnetic effect of the organisation's brand in recruiting the right talent. For example, a reputation for leading a well-run organisation, enlightened thinking about how to manage people, and a willingness to invest in them can all be potent factors in attracting talent.

Rewarding and challenging work

High potentials, particularly recent graduates, often complain their work is boring or non-stimulating. Word soon gets around about dull situations. Pay particular attention to ensuring your employees have meaningful, rewarding work.

 Tip

Identify the riskiest, most challenging positions across the organisation and assign them directly to your rising stars.

Personalised development plans

Knowing the organisation insists on personalised development plans attracts talent. The best plans are usually joint creations between individuals and their talent manager.

 Tip

Link these plans to the organisation's own plans for growth, rather than to some abstract competency framework.

Social networking and working collaboratively

What does your organisation think about social networking and the whole move towards collaborative working? This can prove a vital factor in whether younger applicants feel attracted by your culture.

Consider setting up or supporting social networks to attract and help retain talent. Be wary of trying to control these and instead set a general tone, for example, the 'network is not a place to mess around'.

The University of Bournemouth established a Facebook site to make contact with past alumni of its computer animation degrees. It attracted over 160 alumni, many now working in the world's leading studios like Weta, ILM and Framestore.

The result was the creation of a jobs forum where ex-students swap news, professional tips, and post job alerts to former colleagues.

Ethics and corporate social responsibility (CSR)

Corporate social responsibility and sound business ethics can help increase the strength to which your organisation becomes a magnet for talent. The reverse is also true. Once a strong magnet for talent, BP, for instance, may have suffered a serious blow to its long-term attractiveness as an employer by downgrading its previous green credentials as a result of the catastrophic oil spill in the Gulf of Mexico.

Coaching and mentoring

These supportive activities assure high potentials that the organisation really is interested in and committed to their personal growth and development. For example, Greater Manchester Police pairs individuals being fast-tracked for leadership with experienced senior officers who act as coaches. The two meet for a day a month to discuss issues of concern. These are often complex situations such as how to handle emotional responses to traumatic events, prioritising a seemingly overwhelming case load, or exerting personal authority.

As a talent manager, do you value the coaching role and its ability to influence individual performance? Or are you a sceptic who regards coaching as something of an expensive luxury? There is evidence that companies that invest in coaching people perform significantly better than those without coaching.

Mentoring, where one person champions and supports a specific individual, is another way of increasing your organisation's magnetism to talent. Mentoring can bypass a difficult chain of command or mitigate the effects of a weak line manager.

Sound recruitment strategies

These days, being an effective talent manager means moving from being a reactive to a proactive recruiter. For example, Baringa Partners, with 130,000 staff and winners of the Best Workplaces in the UK, 2010 competition has a culture that deliberately focuses on supporting and growing talented and motivated staff. To achieve this all the senior staff are involved in every recruiting decision the company makes.

Sound recruitment strategies involve increasingly sophisticated and varied methods to find the right talent. The methods go far beyond conventional recruitment agencies, head hunting, the university milk round, recruitment fairs or basic advertisements in traditional media. For instance, there has been a major switch in tactics to using websites and social networking to bring recruiters into contact with prospective employees. Gen Y students, for example, fed on a diet of the internet and Facebook now expect to see video blogs and online diaries of role models from organisations to which they are considering applying. They would also expect to be able to send messages to a recruiter and receive information by email or chat room and to see vacancies displayed on jobs boards. They might also set up on their PCs 'alerts' which notify them instantly of a vacancy or of an interview date.

 Tips

Other actions by talent-hungry recruiters include:

- **appointing specialised recruitment managers**
- **consolidating recruitment efforts on a global scale**
- **raising the company profile and aggressively brand building**
- **identifying new talent pools including entire countries**
- **building long-term relationships with universities and technical schools**
- **turning workforce planning into a strategic weapon**
- **looking for new recruitment technologies**
- **improving candidate selection methods.**

These are new realities for many talent managers and may mean letting go of some old-style thinking about talent.

Old reality	New reality
Recruiting is like purchasing	Recruiting is like sales and marketing: the organisation is the product
Recruit from traditional sources	Look at diverse pools of talent and be prepared to train and develop
People accept offers	People demand much more
Recruit to fill today's vacant positions	Hunt for talent all the time, and plan much further ahead

Talented candidates themselves are defining a number of issues they consider important, and which are pivotal to companies wanting to hire and retain them. These include the work–life balance, professional development programmes, family considerations and values, as well as new ideas about retirement.

In a MetLife benefits study,[2] more than half of the respondents rated work–life balance as a key job selection criterion, with a similar percentage of men and women saying it was a critical factor for them. Another indication of changing

[2] MetLife (2009) '8th Annual Study of Employee Benefits Trends. Findings from the National Survey of Employers and Employees'.

attitudes and priorities is that over half of those polled said they 'will actively seek to work for an organisation whose purpose or mission they agree with'.[3]

Talent managers who adapt to the new reality of talent recruitment by understanding the issues and developing strategies will be the clear winners. Because the scene is constantly evolving, you need to keep checking on the zeitgeist, staying alert to what seems most likely to get through to the right people.

There is also an increasing trend for entire industries to try to influence the quality of their future workforce by becoming involved in designing academic syllabi, providing placements and even sending senior executives to run seminars with students.

Canny employers are not waiting for talent to surface, but are skimming off the best graduates through a form of pre-university milk round. For instance, for skills in short supply, employers offer sponsorship with modest grants to help chosen students pay their way through university and emerge relatively debt free. The relationship is further strengthened through offers of summer vacation paid internships.

Nurture

A reputation for nurturing talent can strongly influence whether talent comes knocking on your door. Make sure there is a wide-ranging approach to encouraging talent with many possible actions available.

The 2009 government report, 'Engaging for Success', by David MacLeod and Nita Clarke, suggested four key cultivators of talent management:

1 a strong strategic leadership
2 a strong strategic narrative
3 an employee voice
4 integrity.[4]

'People leave managers not organisations,' goes the familiar saying, and too many of those with responsibility for getting the best from people do not regard themselves as talent managers at all. They may be excellent salespeople, doctors, lawyers, journalists or IT programmers. Yet when it comes to handling people they fall at the first hurdle by not seeing themselves as there to unlock people's potential.

Nurturing talent requires talent managers to understand the essentials of engagement, what it takes to **V**alue, **I**nvolve, **D**evelop and **I**nspire people. In short, there needs to be a VIDI culture (see Figure 5.3) which we explore further in Chapter 6.

[3] Ibid.
[4] David MacLeod and Nita Clarke (2009) 'Engaging for Success: Enhancing performance through employee engagement' A report to Government, Office of Public Sector Information, Information Policy Team.

Figure 5.3 The VIDI culture

Source: Maynard Leigh Associates.

Every organisation has a culture, a set of implicit beliefs or 'the way we do things round here'. Sometimes these are expressed through a mission statement or a set of leadership core values. Even without those explicit statements, effective leaders are good on narrative, able to tell their staff and customers 'where we have come from, where we are now, and where we are going'.

A common complaint from graduates is of being ignored by those in charge of talent. For example, in some companies, after a two-year training programme moving around the organisation they simply fall off the radar. They arrive in a no-man's land between the end of the training programme and their first real post of seniority. Without a talent-minded manager or mentor, career progression ends up being left entirely to chance.

 Tip

Consider building in more formal continuous professional development (CPD).

For example, in the UK, around a third of newly qualified teachers give up teaching within their first three years. Having passed their probationary year in a school and becoming newly qualified, most receive no further career development. Left to sink or swim, record numbers choose to exit the profession.

In 2010 the UK's teachers' Training and Development Agency for Schools launched a Masters degree in teaching and learning. Newly qualified teachers were invited to apply and schools were fully funded to release teachers to study part-time for a new professional qualification based on their classroom practice and supervised by a learning mentor in their own school. The new employee message had become: 'we want to nurture your talent'.

Nurturing talent is not something 'done to someone' it is a continuous process of fine tuning across the organisation, not restricted to HR departments. Ideally, nurturing talent needs to become embedded from the boardroom down, a key part of an organisation's strategic vision. It is everyone's responsibility.

Nurturing talent

'Talent isn't just confined to the top 20 per cent,' comments Sarah Myers, HR and Talent Management Director for the 16,000 strong BskyB group. 'We continually challenge people to be the best they can be.'

Not so long ago, Britannia Building Society actively nurtured only its rising stars. Now the company cascades its leadership development model throughout the organisation to encourage individuals at all levels to raise their game. HR Director Adrian Powell explains: 'Initially it was the top 100 leaders but it's now been broadened out to 5,000 staff.' Britannia has evolved a nurturing policy around talent and succession which means the organisation identifies and grows individuals who can make the required progress through the organisation.

Tesco welcomes school leavers and nurtures talent from its general store management intake, offering to sponsor the most promising candidates to take a foundation degree in retailing, after watching how they perform in the job.

Burger chain McDonald's also takes a keen interest in its talent. As part of an incentive-driven culture the company has set up what is called the Hamburger University where staff can learn techniques of fast-food management from seasoned practitioners.

Retain

In mid-2010 two of America's biggest modelling agencies went for each other's throats, accusing the other of 'talent theft'. One went further, taking court action against its rival, saying the latter had run a campaign to raid its valuable collection of top models.[5] Next Models of New York alleged that its rival Next Management had poached no fewer than six of its top models, including one described as 'the most important young model to emerge on the fashion scene for years and the next Cindy Crawford'.

Hanging onto your talent is as important as recruiting it in the first place. The reasons people work for an organisation are quite different from what keeps them working there. 'We are at the earliest stage of understanding the challenges of finding, keeping and engaging talent in a genuinely global and intensely competitive business,' reported a 2006 Towers Perrin study.[6]

[5] Ed Pilkington (2010), 'Model wars break out', *Guardian*, 22 May.
[6] See note 1.

Research shows that you can expect a high retention rate if your organisation's culture values and nurtures talented employees. As the Towers Perrin report authors put it: 'People want to work for companies that approach talent in this way and view people as critical to their success.'[7] More specifically the top five drivers of retention globally are:

1 the organisation retains people with the necessary skills
2 satisfaction with the organisation's decisions
3 my manager understands what motivates me
4 an ability to balance my work–personal life
5 the reputation of the organisation as a good employer.

In the UK what also contributes to high retention rates are when the salary criteria are fair and consistent, the overall quality of supervision and whether savings/ pension will provide sufficient income in retirement to meet an individual's needs.

 Tip

It makes sound economic sense to pay attention to your organisation's retention rates: think what it costs to replace someone you value in your organisation.

In the oil business, for instance, it costs around $60,000 to replace an employee. With 25,000 employees and a 20% attrition rate an oil firm could pay an astronomical $30 million to replace lost talent. Do you know the current attrition rate in your organisation and what it costs?

Is yours a talent-intensive organisation? If it relies on having talented people to succeed, they will almost certainly be mobile and, even in difficult trading times, probably find it relatively easy to move elsewhere. When talented people find themselves temporarily locked in because of poor economic conditions, they will almost certainly explode outwards when the situation changes, which it can do with dizzying speed.

The old aim of simply minimising the number of people who leave is being widely replaced with a new one of influencing who leaves and when. In practical terms you need a retention strategy. In a well-known global consultancy, for example, rather than wait for attrition rates to take their toll, the firm operates a clear if brutal policy of 'up or out'. That is, if you are not progressing fast enough you will be asked to leave.

A retention strategy need not be hard to devise or particularly complex. The basic step, as previously explained, is deciding what you mean by 'talent' and

[7] Ibid.

whether you are referring to the few or the many. Secondly, review how your organisation decides that someone is exceptional. Is it just knowledge or attitude, or an approach to getting things done? How can you best help such people succeed?

Thirdly, use the VIDI framework (see above) to promote retention, and before attrition sets in. What will it take, for example, for your talent to feel valued – really appreciated and recognised?

> ### Deterring high attrition rates amongst teachers
>
> - **Teachers given extra staff time to prepare for the assessment process.**
> - **External invigilators hired to save teachers staffing examination venues.**
> - **Reprographics officers hired to photocopy work and prepare resources.**
> - **A behaviour officer appointed to undertake some pastoral duties.**
> - **A shortened school day but with an earlier start.**
> - **Reduce the number of reports issued a year, whilst still meeting statutory guidelines.**
> - **Parents' evenings scheduled straight after school, so staff still have some of their evening left.**

Mistakes by talent managers that can lead to losing talent are both well researched and avoidable. For example, an international study in 2009[8] of more than 20,000 employees dubbed as 'rising stars' in more than 100 international organisations revealed that many talent management programmes simply don't deliver much in the way of results. Around 40% of internal job moves by people identified by their companies as 'high potentials' end in failure. At the heart of this failure lies a lack of engagement but with these additional sobering facts:

- One in four high potentials intend to leave within the year.
- One in three admits to not putting their effort into the job.
- One in five believes their personal aspirations are quite different from what the organisation planned for them.
- Four out of 10 have little confidence in their co-workers and even less confidence in the senior team.[9]

[8] Jean Martin and Conrad Schmidt 'How to keep your top talent', *Harvard Business Review*, May 2010.
[9] Ibid.

Behind these lethal statistics undermining talent retention, lie avoidable mistakes by talent managers. One of these is having outsized expectations of what the most talented people can deliver. Similarly, many high potentials set incredibly high standards for their companies to achieve, so when the company is struggling, the star players tend to be the first to be disappointed.

 Six mistakes that may doom your talent investment

- Assume that high potentials are highly engaged.
- Equate current high performance with future potential.
- Delegate down the management of top talent.
- Shield rising stars from early derailment.
- Expect star employees to share the pain.
- Fail to link stars to your corporate strategy.

Source: Jean Martin and Conrad Schmidt 'How to keep your top talent',
Harvard Business Review, May 2010.

Action on retention

Based on the experience of successful talent managers, here are some practical actions you can take to reduce attrition rates and encourage the retention of talent within your organisation:

- **Engagement:** discover and focus on levels of engagement, ensuring your people feel valued, involved, developed and inspired (VIDI).
- **Test:** develop ways to measure potential so you can target scarce resources. Consider measuring three dimensions essential for talent retention: ability, engagement and aspiration.
- **Relationship:** promote good relationships at work since many excellent retention rates are due to the strength of the ones created within the organisation. In particular, people feel valued where there is trust and they have the autonomy they need to be effective.

- **Communication:** review the quality of communication across your organisation. For example, to what extent do team members know their roles, job description and responsibilities within the organisation? Do people feel 'in the loop' and informed about current issues?

- **Job design:** make sure job designs contribute to retention rather than attrition. When UPS studied why drivers left, they found that the turnover could be traced to the exhausting task of loading the trucks at the beginning of their shift. Hiring and training drivers is time-consuming and expensive, so UPS set out to reduce driver turnover by changing the job design. The company hired a whole new set of employees to load trucks. The turnover in that particular loading job is now 400% a year, but it's easier to fill those positions than to find reliable drivers. The company did not increase overall retention, it just reduced turnover where it counted.

- **Feedback:** rather than wait for an annual performance evaluation, give regular feedback on how an employee is performing. Regular means anything from daily, weekly to monthly. Talented people in particular like frequent feedback about how they are performing. Shortening the feedback loop helps keep performance levels high and reinforces positive behaviours.

- **Compensation package:** recognise your star players by offering truly differentiated compensation arrangements. People want to feel they are being paid appropriately and fairly for the work done. Research the salaries and benefits that other organisations offer, including regional and national compensation averages.

  Your people will soon know if your compensation package is uncompetitive. Don't wait for them to uncover the reality and start sniffing around for better terms.

- **Work–life balance:** show that you care about the work–life balance of your people. In 1999, only 40% of BP staff, for example, thought that the work–life balance was well managed and acceptable to them. By 2002 that figure had risen to 65%, which puts the company in the top 10% of companies surveyed. No amount of money will retain an employee if work puts a significant strain on the family. Small gestures, such as allowing a team member to take an extended lunch once a week to watch his son's baseball game, will be repaid with loyalty and extended employment with an organisation.

- **Growth opportunities:** keep a constant look out for growth opportunities for your talent. If someone seems bored or burned out in a current position offer to develop them in another facet of the organisation where they would be a good fit.

- **Recognition:** use appreciation lavishly. It's the cheapest talent retention technique and the least used. A short email or stopping by a team member's desk and saying 'thanks' can do wonders for morale. Other options might include a mention in the company newsletter for outstanding performance or gift certificates to a restaurant or movie theatre – the possibilities are endless.

- **Define expectations:** tackle any vagueness about what your people are supposed to be doing in their jobs. Being unsure about what is expected of you at work is a sure way to encourage dissatisfaction and possible departure.

- **Equity:** good retention practice often amounts to ensuring transparency such as how decisions are made about developing people, and in treating people equally without undue favouritism.

- **Volunteers:** treat employees as partners rather than cannon fodder or hired hands. Assume your people are volunteers and can walk at any time. Progressive companies ditch time clocks.

- **Encourage social interaction:** encourage the development of social ties among employees. For instance, Ingage Solutions has held turnover of software engineers to 7% mainly by developing initiatives that create a social community.

 Creating a talent retention culture

- **VIDI framework:** the organisation pursues implications of VIDI (see above).
- **Effective teams:** high potentials are part of groups not isolated.
- **Expertise and competence:** these are valued more than rank or status.
- **Mutual respect:** people recognise the contribution of colleagues who support them.
- **Respected leadership:** people see leadership that makes a difference.
- **Openness:** autonomy, space, trust and flexibility become second nature.
- **Risk taking:** failure is merely a way of learning, and people are constantly encouraged to try new things.
- **Engagement is expected:** the level of commitment from people is high and constantly monitored.
- **Promote from within:** buying in talent is always a last, not a first, resort.
- **Work–life balance:** people can have a viable working day with space for the rest of their life too.

The women in your life

Though women consist of nearly half the workforce they make up less than 10% of top executive talent. Depending on your point of view, this is either a scandalous waste of talent or somehow a natural order of things.

Smart talent managers reject the under-use of women in their organisations and work hard to counteract it. Talented women leave organisations not merely because of the notorious glass ceiling, i.e. blocks to success, but also because:

- they see it is smarter to start their own businesses
- the employer does not offer the degree of flexibility they need in their lives.

 Retaining female talent

In order to retain your female talent:

- **Offer flexible work arrangements.** More and more women (and men) are seeking this. Offer this to your employees and watch your retention rates climb.
- **Start or expand formal mentoring programmes.** There are many benefits to both women and the organisation from enabling them to learn from seasoned professionals. With good mentoring not only do talented women get up to speed faster they acquire a broader organisational perspective, and expand internal contacts for getting things done faster with and through others.
- **Promote women to senior-level positions.** There is a sound business case for developing women into the management ranks and adding them to the executive suite. Companies with the highest percentages of women corporate officers have, on average, a 35.1% higher return on equity and 34% more total return to shareholders than companies with the lowest percentages.[10]

Demographics

Are you fully demographic aware? Talent management requires an awareness of people trends and, in particular, who will be available to be employed when needed.

In the western world, for example, there are now fewer people of working age, that is, from 15 to 64 (see Figure 5.4). This is creating global movements of jobs and populations as companies seek to fill skill and labour needs. Most of the 2020 workforce has already left school. To ignore the needs of older workers therefore means missing out on a huge group of people who can adapt to new jobs and new roles. Lifelong learning and continuing education are therefore going to be important factors in maintaining skills and talent into the future.

Slow population growth rates in developed nations, ageing populations, baby boomers reaching retirement, are all expected to influence not only who is available to recruit but also retentions. In the UK, for example, the average age of public sector employees is 48 and rising. Even with projected radical changes in

[10] US Banker (2008) 'The 25 Most Powerful Women in Banking: The calm amid the storm', by Holly Sraeel, online at www.americanbanker.com.

Figure 5.4 Percentage change in the working-age population (aged 15 to 64), 2005 to 2025

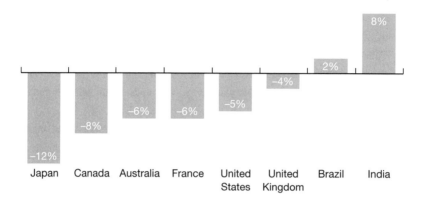

Source: World Population Prospects (2005). Population division of the Dept of Economic and Social Affairs of the United Nations Secretariat.

the size of the public sector made by the new government in 2010, there will be skills shortages on a massive scale unless training and recruitment are stepped up to ease the transition. In the NHS in Scotland, retirement rates of administrative staff are destined to take a serious toll on skills and knowledge.

Paint a picture

What attracts, nurtures and retains talent is awareness that one is part of an exciting present and an attractive future. So an essential skill of every talent manager is the ability to articulate clearly what the organisation is doing and to what it aspires.

Unlocking people's potential, particularly of talented individuals, is all about painting a picture of the future and providing inspiration. Being able to describe the future in exciting and compelling ways is the bedrock of effective talent management. For this reason an increasing number of organisations are investing in the art of storytelling, helping their talent managers to bring the future to life.

How good is your storytelling? Can you articulate the future for your talented people in ways that excite and inspire? Emphasising the future puts talent in its proper perspective. Your talent management must challenge your rising stars, not just celebrate their recent successes. After all, the future of the organisation is in their hands.

Briefing lessons

- The seven key steps to implementing talent management are: define, clarify, identify, design, develop, implement and evaluate.
- Rather than becoming over-focused on these steps, pursue four imperatives for making talent management viable: be a magnet for talent (recruit), cultivate talent (nurture), hang onto your talent (retain) and deal with the people trends (demographics).
- In tackling the recruitment of talent it is important to give attention to the organisation's brand and to ensuring effective people practices. The latter consists of seven areas of activity: effective management, interesting and rewarding work, personalised development plans, networking and collaboration, ethics and CSR, coaching and mentoring, and sound recruitment strategies.
- There are new realities for many talent managers to consider and this may mean letting go of old-style thinking about talent.
- Establishing a reputation for nurturing talent strongly influences whether it comes knocking on the organisation's door. In particular, nurturing talent requires managers to understand the essentials of engagement and what it takes to value, involve, develop and inspire people (VIDI).
- Retaining talent is as important as recruiting it in the first place. The reasons why people find themselves attracted to an organisation are different to why they tend to stay working for it.
- Globally, the top five drivers of retention are 1) the organisation retains people with needed skills, 2) satisfaction with organisational decisions, 3) managers understand each person and what motivates them, 4) the ability of people to balance their work and personal life, and 5) the reputation of the organisation as a good employer.
- There are six mistakes that may doom the investment in talent management (see p. 75) but we list a series of practical actions that talent managers can take to reduce attrition rates and encourage retention.
- Demographics are playing an increasingly influential role in the ability to recruit and retain talent. It is important that talent managers make themselves aware of these trends and what they mean for who will be available when needed.
- There is one more skill that talent managers need to master: the ability to paint a picture of the future to explain what the organisation is doing and to what it aspires.

How to manage talent

6

Introduction

Leaders have worried over it for centuries and perhaps millennia. How do you get the best from people, especially from those you regard as talented?

Opening the door to someone's talent requires not merely a key, but the right one. It is important to distinguish between high performance and high potential: they are not always the same. So in managing talent you will need to focus your attention on how to help people

- perform well
- achieve peak performance.

The first requires that your people feel fully engaged with their work. The second requires them to go beyond engagement, to hit their absolute best.

Peak performance is rather like a controlled explosion. As a talent manager you can help light the fuse that triggers someone achieving their best, sometimes much to their surprise. It needs a definite starting point and happens when people use their potential to excel.

Engagement

In 2010 Dr Judith Bardwick of Durham Business School identified a worrying trend in the UK workplace. A growing number of employers or organisations were failing to respond to employees in ways that confirm that they are of value. Dr Bardwick refers to the phenomenon as 'emotional or psychological recession'.[1]

Talent managers should not simply go through the motions of coaching and helping employees improve – they should actually mean it. Emotional engagement follows when employees feel they are making a difference. Engaged employees are more productive. They are also more profitable, more customer-focused, safer, and more likely to withstand temptations to leave. The best-performing companies know that raising engagement levels and linking this to corporate goals will help them win in the marketplace.

[1] Cited in Andrea Adams (2010) 'Changing Role of HR', LexisNexis, 1 June.

Engaged employees

- **Work at up to three times the rate of the disengaged (William James, Harvard).[2]**
- **Take less than half the sickness absence days, 2.7 compared with 6.2 (Gallup).[3]**
- **Are 87% less likely to leave (Corporate Leadership Council).[4]**
- **Are far more likely to speak well of the employer to others, 67% compared with 3% (Gallup)[5]**

In fact, companies with engaged employees are said to have nearly four times the earnings per share (EPS) growth rate, compared to those with lower engagement in their same industry.[6] Unfortunately, only about a quarter of UK employees feel really engaged with their job, according to the 2010 Gallup survey. No wonder that the UK's employers' union, the CBI, warned that employee engagement is now the biggest challenge facing employers.

An earlier 2005 study by Towers Perrin also found that: 'In most countries the vast majority of workers, typically between one-half and three-quarters; are only moderately engaged.'[7] These awkward statistics are a challenge to any talent manager:

- To what extent do you understand the key drivers of engagement?
- What can you do about them?

In seeking the answers to these questions, it is easy to become lost in the thicket of strategy and corporate goals. This is rather like seeing the wood while never noticing the actual trees.

Apart from those in the highest reaches of the organisation, most talent managers need to focus less on the macro world of engagement strategy and more on practical action. That is, finding what will engage each direct report through

---

[2] David MacLeod and Nita Clarke (2009) 'Engaging for Success: Enhancing performance through employee engagement'. A report to Government, Office of Public Sector Information, Information Policy Team.

[3] Ibid.

[4] Ibid.

[5] Ibid.

[6] Gallup (2010), *Employee Engagement*, 17 July.

[7] O'Neal, S. and Gebaver, J. (2006) 'Talent management in the 21st century: Attracting, retaining and engaging employees of choice', *World at Work*, Towers Perrin.

- management style
- smart goals
- coaching and performance reviews
- motivation
- talent identification
- diversity
- relating to Gen Y.

Management style

Achieving high levels of engagement is an art not a science. Effective talent managers therefore learn to adjust their managerial style to suit those whom they are managing.

This ability to respond flexibly depends on possessing or developing a full range of personal expression. Think of it as using a larger palette of colours with different responses, depending on what the situation requires – empathy, humour, insight, patience, curiosity, anger, amusement, determination, directness and so on. Do you need to add some colours to your own range of personal expression?

Tailoring your personal style to meet the needs of your people may also require practice in developing your ability to see what is going on around you. For example, do you correctly interpret what is happening below the surface of people's behaviour or attitudes? Do you feel you understand what they may need to become more engaged and therefore fully use their potential?

Developing a flexible leadership style may come naturally to you, but it may also require some active personal development to exercise this muscle, so it becomes a strength, rather than your weakness.

SMART goals

SMART goals are a reliable way of developing people and taking them to the next level of engagement. These are goals that are: **S**tretching, **M**easurable, **A**ccepted, **R**ecorded and **T**ime-limited.

People usually respond best to SMART goals when they have been involved in choosing them, rather than having them imposed. But as with all 'rules' of human behaviour, there may be occasions when it is right to impose goals as a way of inspiring people to achieve the near impossible.

Coaching and performance review

The best talent managers are excellent coaches. If you feel ill-equipped to be a high-performance coach and to conduct free-ranging performance reviews you are not alone. Many practising managers feel that way too, yet these skills are eminently learnable.

You may find it helpful to attend a coaching event, during which you get to practise different coaching skills and techniques. Managing talent is not a one-way affair in which you map out a course of action for the other person. It is a partnership, where you treat people whose engagement you want to affect with respect and where, for instance, front line staff become empowered to make decisions.

Motivation

A persistent myth about managing talent is that motivation is something you *do* to people. In fact, people possess their own motivators; it's what makes them feel engaged. You cannot simply impose yours onto them.

Each person has a unique collection of motivators, affecting what they think, feel and do. Practical talent management action involves uncovering these and responding to them appropriately

There is a generational aspect to motivation. Generation Y and baby boomers, for example, share a heightened sense of obligation to make a positive contribution to society and the health of the planet. Over 80% say that it is important that their work involves 'giving back'. This is not as true for Gen X, those in their thirties and early forties. They are less likely to find this important.

Being aware of such inner drives is therefore important in building an environment in which young talent can thrive. For example, a lack of a sufficiently flexible working environment is a serious turn off. Having the freedom to choose when and where to work can be a powerful attraction and way of winning their engagement.

Talent identification

As mentioned earlier, work performance is not necessarily the same as using someone's full potential. As a talent manager you will need to go beyond someone's day-to-day performance and explore their under-used abilities. HR mechanisms, such as formal assessment centres, work projects and annual reviews can only take you so far in getting the best from your people. It is also important to get close to each individual whose talent you want to unlock.

A strong relationship with direct reports will help you acquire the necessary insight into what unused talent might be available. The more distance you place between you and this talent the harder it becomes to tap into it when you need that person to go the extra mile, to perform at their best.

Start by drawing up a list of your people's talents. The very act of having to write down the evidence may push you into spending more time with these people to discover what you need to know. You are seeking answers to such questions as:

- To what extent are we using your full potential?
- What more could you do given the opportunity?

- Can you see how we can do things better round here?
- What, if anything, gets in the way of you performing even better?
- How could I make it easier for you to do your job better?

Talent management also means putting the right people in the right place so it is possible to utilise their full potential.

Diversity

Astute managers on the lookout for talent realise that exploiting the benefits of diversity can be an untapped source of creativity, provide a competitive advantage and insight into a wider range of customers.

Perhaps the most blatant under-use of talent concerns the failure to use the potential of women. In top jobs across whole swathes of the economy, notably in construction, science, engineering, technology, manufacturing, defence and finance, men continue to outnumber women by around 10 to one.

The UK construction industry has long had a problem with using women's talent. A 2006 report[8], for example, found that less than one in 10 construction workers were women and of these 83% were in secretarial roles! IT is yet another industry with an unsatisfactory and disproportionate number of male managers. Here women-friendly policies can have a big impact in nurturing individual talent, as Npower and the Abingdon-based education software company RM discovered.

RM and Npower: unlocking female talent

One in three of the company's graduate intake and one in four front line staff are women. Indeed, women occupy at least three senior board positions. The company's success at unlocking its female talent is partly due to its women-friendly, flexible hours of working, allowing them to manage childcare and achieve a better work–life balance.

Similarly, 40% of NPower's workforce is now women, but most are concentrated in sales and customer service. The company is committed to increasing its number of women professionals and in 2010 five out of seven of its graduate engineering roles were filled by women.

Pay inequality between men and women remains a huge turn-off for talent. There is an urgent need to foster more transparency and fairer deals for women in many organisations. Soon companies may find themselves compelled by legislation to reveal what they pay women and men, with the obligation to take positive action to promote diversity.

[8] The Chartered Institute to Building, 'Inclusivity: the Changing Role of Women in the Construction Workforce (2006).

Forty decades after the UK introduced equal pay legislation, women still earn on average a fifth less than men. For the astute talent manager this represents an opportunity to steal a march on less wised-up colleagues. By looking closely at the pay of your female staff, for example, you may well uncover an under-exploited tool for attracting and unlocking talent.

More broadly, organisations are still learning how to be more inclusive in respect of sexual orientation, physical and mental disability, ageism and so on, as well as gender differences. Tapping the talents of disabled groups, for example, offers many creative possibilities and talent managers in some companies are taking action to meet four formal commitments: the employment, retention, training and career development of disabled employees.

 Tips

- **Interview all applicants with a disability who meet the minimum criteria for a job vacancy and consider them on their abilities.**
- **Ensure there is a mechanism in place to discuss, at any time, but at least once a year, with disabled employees what you and they can do to make sure they can develop and use their abilities.**
- **Make every effort when employees become disabled to ensure they stay in employment.**
- **Take action to ensure that all employees develop the appropriate level of disability awareness needed to make your commitments work.**
- **Each year, review the above four commitments and what has been achieved, plan ways to improve on them and let employees and the Employment Service know about progress and future plans.**

Diversity remains an area where much talent is wasted and this will continue until firms transform their daily practices.

 Tips

- **Treat others with respect.**
- **Avoid using stereotypes.**
- **Make it clear that prejudice is wrong.**
- **Do not allow bigoted comments by others to go unchallenged.**

Relating to Gen Y

Shaun Orpen aged 26 is a typical high achieving Gen Y. He has been actively shaping his career through frequent moves: 'In the last seven years I've had four jobs. I started as a trainee insurance broker, moving up the ladder to become a commercial broker which kept me stretched. But then I realised that promotion depended on dead men's shoes. I moved to London and switched to software sales.'

It has been said that 'a career is crazy paving you lay yourself' and Gen Y people like Shaun are acutely aware of it. Realising there is no job for life, this new workforce phenomenon expects to move around and not remain stuck in one place for decades. For example, a report in April 2008 by specialist development consultancy Talentsmoothie[9] on what Gen Y wants, claimed that Gen Y is 'fundamentally different' from its counterparts, Gen X and the post-war baby boomers.

Over half of those interviewed expected to stay less than two years in their first job, while 44% on their second job did not expect to remain in it longer than five years. Similarly, a recent US government survey[10] predicted that a typical Gen Y would have up to 10 jobs before the age of 38. While this figure may well be reduced by recession, it does reflect an increased appetite for change.

Employers have always been prepared to invest in individuals who they want to fast track. But with the rise of Gen Y there is a new approach to talent emerging. Organisations encourage individuals to take far more responsibility for their own career development.

Generation Y places greater demands on those who must manage their talent. For example, they are demanding managers they can relate to and careers they can feel passionate about. As digital natives they embrace social networking, blogs and wikis and use them naturally as part of their work. Getting the best from such people demands talent managers who embrace such ideas.

Happy Computers: catering for Gen Y

IT training company Happy Computers has built an inclusive culture around Generation Y. Chief executive Henry Stewart says:

I think the difference between Gen Y and other groups can be over-hyped. The key to a happy workplace is involving as many people in developing the key skills needed to run the business.

Generation Y may react most strongly against command and control management but it doesn't work for any age group. And all benefit from better work–life balance.

---

[9] talentsmoothie, 'Generation Y: What They Want From Work' (April 2008).
[10] US Census for the Bureau of Labor.

A further implication of the Gen Y phenomenon is that talent managers may need to revisit and revise the psychological contract they have with their staff. Once, there was a strong, implied duty of care and obligation by a company towards its employees. With the rise of talent that votes with its feet, all bets are off, as both sides negotiate more flexible arrangements. For example, long-term job security may be dead, but in its place comes more people-centred HR policies, including rewards linked more tightly to performance.

Axa: connecting with a younger internal and external market

 Generation Y has been a profound influence on insurance group Axa, so that it has shifted its communications to aim at a more technology savvy group.

Sonia Wolsey-Cooper, Axa's HR Director, argues that Gen Y expectations are 'different and their attention span is shorter.

> *We're becoming much more visual rather than aural. You need a punchier message. Young people are looking for high-impact experiences. They are punchy, vocal and vying for attention. That feeds through into society. It all builds up to a slightly different attitude to the world of work.*

> *The challenge for us is to marry the expectations of a diverse workforce from people who've been with us for 30 years right through to new grad intake. We've come up with a healthy culture that all can buy into without any sector feeling excluded.*

Learning from its Gen Y talent is also helping Axa connect with a younger market, as Wolsey-Cooper says:

> *Generation Y has forced us to look at our external brand. Generation Y are keen to find out about the values of the organisation and how it operates socially. That's very difficult. I think organisations should be challenging the way they do business and their roots in society and the environment.*

Engagement drivers

Since staff engagement is a core part of talent management, this route to utilising people's potential has received considerable attention, particularly since a UK government-sponsored report on the topic emerged in late 2009.[11] A staff survey is one way of understanding the engagement drivers within an organisation and by implication the sort of remedial action leaders might need to consider.

[11] David MacLeod and Nita Clarke (2009) 'Engaging for Success: Enhancing perform-ance through employee engagement'. A report to Government, Office of Public Sector Information, Information Policy Team.

For instance, Gallup pioneered its Q12 questionnaire to provide a framework for measuring engagement and by implication appropriate leadership action.

In world-class organisations, for every eight fully engaged people Gallup claims there is one who is not. By contrast the average is closer to 1:5. That is, for every engaged person there are five who are disengaged. Gallup's engagement ratio is a broad indicator of an organisation's health.

Mercer, another respected research organisation, uses a slightly different approach to clarifying engagement drivers at work. Its global variables include:

- opportunities for development
- confidence and trust in leadership
- recognition and rewards
- organisational communication.[12]

Interestingly, in contrast to other research, Mercer claims engagement drivers differ across nations. For example, in the US the top three reasons people feel engaged are:

- confident they can achieve career objectives
- a sense of personal accomplishment
- confident that the organisation will be successful.[13]

By contrast, in the UK the top three drivers are:

- a sense of personal accomplishment
- confidence in senior management
- opportunities for training.[14]

While there are numerous ways of measuring employee engagement, there is usually less emphasis in helping talent managers decide what to do about it. It's as if asking people to answer a survey questionnaire is enough. Having completed a survey many managers convince themselves they have actually engaged with their employees. But as one wit summed up the issue: 'No one ever got a pig fat by weighing it.'

---

[12] Mercer (2007) 'Point of View: Engaging employees to drive global business success', 27 November, online at www.mercer.com/whatsworking
[13] Ibid.
[14] Ibid.

VIDI

The VIDI framework, developed by Maynard Leigh Associates, offers a slightly different tool for focusing on engagement drivers and what it takes to unlock people's potential. It assumes managers must learn to 'see' what is needed in each situation.

The VIDI framework has four basic areas in which to assess and influence engagement. To achieve high levels of engagement employees need to feel **V**alued, **I**nvolved, **D**eveloped and **I**nspired (see Figure 6.2). Usable also as a questionnaire, this framework provides a disciplined way of getting to grips with what any one individual might need to fully use their potential.

Figure 6.2

Source: © Maynard Leigh Associates.

The four VIDI drivers roughly match the universal drivers of engagement drawn from occupational psychological research.[15]

Valued

One of the deepest hungers of the human heart is to be seen and to be understood. In simple terms, to feel valued. This is particularly so when people feel alienated and disassociated from the world. To feel valued employees must feel that their individuality counts, they actually experience the benefits of positive relationships and recognise that they are treated fairly.

'Feeling good while you are doing something is a sign of optimal cognitive efficiency or doing a good job,' argues renowned psychologist, author and researcher Daniel Goleman. His book on emotional intelligence has widely influenced perceptions of the task of talent management. Goleman argues that at an emotional level the job of a leader or manager is helping 'people to get and stay in the specific brain state where they can work at their best. It requires social intelligence. One of the ways leaders do this all the time, whether they know it or not, is through emotional intelligence.'[16]

There are many facets to emotional intelligence. One of the most important is being able to recognise or interpret people's motivators and to respond appropriately. Though this kind of intelligence is learnable it also comes with maturity.

[15] The Training Foundation (2010) *The Rules of Engagement*.
[16] Daniel Goleman (1995) *Emotional Intelligence: Why it can matter more than IQ*, Batam.

Involved

At whatever level you are in the organisation as a leader you are expected to create a sense of involvement and rapport with your people. In some companies, such as Fedex, this is continuously assessed and if your scores are too low you will be called to account. Score low two months running and you may be relegated to a less-demanding role.

The idea of involving employees in how a business is run has been happening since 1771, when William Denny introduced to a Glasgow shipyard the first employee suggestion scheme. Most organisations have progressed beyond this basic level of involvement, but despite a mass of evidence proving its benefits many fall short in this area.

In their seminal book *Built to Last* (2004), Collins and Porras reported that businesses seeking an active involvement by their employees had a massive 16-to-1 long-term stockmarket differential, compared to those organisations that did not.

Similarly, Buckingham and Coffman at Gallup surveyed over 1 million employees and 80,000 managers worldwide and found that positive employee involvement correlated directly with business profitability.[17]

Employee involvement happens when people feel they can have an impact on decisions and actions that affect their jobs. This is neither a goal nor a tool. Rather it is a philosophy about how people are most enabled to contribute to continuous improvement and the ongoing success of their work organisation.

The O2 company, for example, employs a 'Head of Employee Involvement' while at M&S the retailer's business involvement group (BIG) gives employees an opportunity to voice their views and ideas. The John Lewis partnership has similarly long regarded involvement as a key resource for achieving talent engagement and for creating a hard to match competitive advantage.

To promote involvement companies sometimes see benefits in encouraging staff to reach out to help in places beyond the organisation, for example where they can make a valuable community contribution. At GSK, for example:

> *We encourage our employees to become involved with deserving causes in their local communities around the globe. We support their time and dedication with various internal programmes and opportunities to encourage active employee involvement.*[18]

In the quest for involvement, managers have often placed excessive reliance on employee surveys. But if you need a survey to discover what your people are thinking you are probably not close enough to them in the first place.

---

[17] Jeremy Starling (2007/2008) 'Why engagement is no longer enough', *Strategic Communication Management*, Dec/Jan, BNET.

[18] www.gsk.com/community/employee_involvement.htm

Involvement at LV=

After listening to members, customers and employees, the management of Liverpool Victoria, a UK insurance company, decided its brand needed to become more relevant. Once the new look, brand name, LV=, and values had been agreed, it was crucial that all employees worked out what this meant for them as individuals.

The company created four powerful, intensive and fun, active half-day experiences to sell the 'what' and the 'why' of the proposed changes. Involvement really started when employees were split into groups and put through a series of active experiences that enabled them to acquire a deeper understanding of the behaviours, values and actions behind the new brand. Visualisers, graffiti and storyboard artists worked with each group to capture their top-level ideas for bringing the new brand to life in their daily work. Giant murals were created live at the events and then put on permanent display in prominent locations at the company's Bournemouth head office.

The success of the employee involvement project included:

- All at LV= now have ownership of a very successful 'external' rebrand.
- New business in life and general insurance, as well as general insurance renewals, are all up year on year.
- There is a 2% fall in employee turnover year on year.
- A 23% improvement in employee understanding of organisational direction.
- A 31% improvement in confidence and motivation by brand, values and behaviours.
- A 21% improvement in commitment to living values and behaviours, and confidence in leadership of the business.

Source: Jeremy Starling, Managing Director of INVOLVE (2007).
'Engagement is not enough,' HR Zone

Developed

As children we cannot help but develop. There is no reason why this should stop the moment we hit adulthood. It is a natural human urge to grow and develop. When talent managers focus on personal development this is a powerful way to engage people at work and to manage their talent. One third or more employees in the UK, though, report that they do not feel they are being developed.[19] This is a considerable amount of wasted human potential.

[19] CIPD (2006) 'Annual Survey: How Engaged are British Employees?'

Development can happen in various ways through formal learning and development, stretch goals, challenging work projects, and promotion to new roles. The best kind of development does not merely give people more skills it also prepares them to perform better and use their potential more fully.

Development is not neutral. It affects how people feel about the organisation and their managers. Done well it builds a vital emotional bond between the individual and the organisation. When people see that you really value the development process it sends a positive message about the importance of engagement and in this way the job of managing talent becomes that much easier.

Development can and often does play a vital role in encouraging people to go that extra mile:

> *Emotional commitment is four times as valuable as rational commitment in producing discretionary effort. Indeed the search for a high performance workforce is synonymous with the search for emotional commitment.*[20]

Inspired

If you want someone to go the extra mile, that is, to do what might otherwise seem impossible or far-fetched, you have to inspire them. It will seldom be enough simply to manage them, to give them direction or a sense of purpose.

The thought of having to inspire people induces a sense of panic in some executives: 'How do I do that?', 'What makes people feel inspired?', 'I know nothing about this thing you call inspiration!' As an abstract ambition, having to inspire others feels daunting or sterile. Why should someone feel inspired by what you say to them or even what you do?

This is probably one of the most challenging areas of talent management to master. Yet, given the right opportunity nearly everyone has the ability to inspire others. In practice, there are many simple actions that leaders and managers do daily that steadily feed people's need for inspiration.

The starting point for inspiring others is first being inspired yourself. This really is the first base. Only by connecting with your own source of inspiration can you expect to affect others who may be thirsting to be inspired themselves. This need to first inspire yourself comes as a surprise to some people and yet it is obvious when you think about it. By contacting your own source of inspiration – perhaps neglected for many years – you gain an important sense of what it takes to tap into other people's need for inspiration.

Developers or coaches who work with managers to show them how to inspire others avoid exhorting them to become inspired. Instead, they ask them to find something from their lives about which they truly felt inspired or uplifted in some way. In a leading Dutch Telecoms company, for example, 18 senior managers needed to prepare for new boardroom roles. At this level, technical know-how and specialist skills were no longer enough. Instead, the company expected them

---

[20] Corporate Leadership Council (2009) *Engaging for Success*.

to show the integrity, passion and belief in the values that their new responsibilities demanded.

These 18 managers attended a learning event where they were free to explore the whole issue of inspiration. Amongst other things it showed them what it means to be inspired. Participants appeared on a theatre stage to share with the group a piece of writing or music that inspired them. As Stuart MacKenzie, Maynard Leigh's Managing Director, explained:

> *One person presented President Obama's inauguration speech; another played us the U2 hit 'Beautiful Day'. We had people recite passages of Shakespeare: one man wrote and performed a poem. The material was used as a vehicle to explore their authentic, inspirational self. They then practised the lessons they had learnt in order to take them back into the workplace so they could inspire their colleagues.*

While the focus is often on leadership providing inspiration to engage people, there may be many other sources that can fuel this feeling. It could be the work they love doing, the cause they are part of, the product or service they supply. As we saw earlier in the GSK example, it could also be in helping on a project in the local community.

Talent managers wanting to promote inspiration therefore have multiple routes to achieve this. Connecting with someone's inspiration is not like turning on a light bulb. Instead, it takes steady nurturing, allowing it to grow within them and to spread and radiate outwards.

Apart from the essential of being inspired yourself, what are some of the other components of successfully inspiring others? How do you bring VIDI alive?

In the next chapter we explore the VIDI framework in more detail to reveal its detailed implications for talent management practice.

Individual peak performance

The great actor, Sir Laurence Olivier, gave many celebrated performances of Othello. On tour one evening in Moscow, something special happened. As usual, the audience showed their appreciation with rapturous applause. But both cast and crew knew that this had been no ordinary performance. Even this recognised and accomplished actor had gone beyond excellence, reaching his peak that evening. Surely it was something to celebrate? However, in his dressing room, Olivier was despondent. When asked why he was so low he replied: 'I know something special happened this evening, but I don't know how I did it!'

In less dramatic ways, each of us probably knows the experience of sometimes being at our best. At other times we know we are falling short. What exactly is the difference between the two? Sports people talk of being 'in the zone', when delivering peak performance. Others, who have hit a particularly golden patch, talk about 'going with the flow'. Paradoxically, when it happens, exceptional performance feels easy, as if everything is going right.

Since around the start of the 20th century, when Frederick Taylor argued for scientific management, the idea of extracting peak performance from people has been undergoing a series of rethinks. Taylorism was more concerned with putting work onto a rational, scientific basis, and completing jobs, than unleashing individual peak performance.

Several decades of this narrow approach produced highly centralised bureaucracies. The resulting rigid, top-down management styles are still seen by workers and managers alike as controlling, conformist and monolithic. More significantly, they do not fully engage people and when this ingredient is missing, peak performance simply does not occur.

No individual, team or company can permanently remain at peak performance. In this sense, even the notion of peak performance becomes questionable. Instead, what organisations usually value more is sustained excellence. Through careful support and other means you may be able to extend the length of time the person performs at their best.

Peak performance can also prove a chimera, an extraordinary, uncontrollable moment never to be repeated. For example, Isaac Newton's revelation about gravity from an apple falling on his head, August Kekule waking from a dream and realising the structure of benzene, Enrico Fermi discovering slow neutrons by 'randomly' substituting a block of paraffin for a tabletop, Alexander Fleming 'accidentally' discovering the action of a famous mould on bacteria, and Werner Heisenberg discovering the awesome structure of the quantum world after an all-night session on the island of Heligoland in the North Sea. Such extraordinary moments may be peaks, yet realistically we cannot expect them to happen often. Instead, sustained excellence in performance may be far more achievable and in some ways desirable.

The challenge for talent managers is how to make the organisation sufficiently attractive to these high level performers that they want to excel and stick around to deliver. Such people, for example, will seldom be impressed by corporate hierarchy, may not want to be led and certainly do not want to be managed. However, potentially outstanding performers need boundaries, simple rules and to be protected from 'organisational rain' or the nonsense of politics and the aggravation of organisational life.

So how can you assist people in your organisation to excel, reaching for, and even beyond their previous personal best? It requires you to actively support the right combination of mental, emotional and practical behaviour (see Figure 6.3).

Figure 6.3 The right combination

think | feel | act | = | perform

Think

Some of the earliest investigation into peak performers by Charles Garfield[21] in the 1980s explored what exactly peak performers do when reaching for their exceptional results. A powerful, if obvious, fact to emerge from Garfield's researches was that peak performers first make a conscious decision to excel. Alongside this comes a personal motivating vision or mission of what their peak performance would look like. Next is their investment in mastering their chosen area of skill and a willingness to keep adapting and learning from how they perform.

Peak performers tend to be mentally highly disciplined people able, for example, to persist at what they are doing long after others have abandoned the chase. You can encourage this mental discipline through your coaching and informed general support. For example, as part of being mentally disciplined, peak performers tend to be mentally highly focused and supremely organised around their chosen goal. Peak performers tend to set themselves demanding and occasionally unreachable goals.[22]

 Tip

Your contribution is to ensure that challenging goals are both achievable and aligned to those of the organisation.

Goal setting often involves creative thinking in which the person constantly strives to look at their task in new ways, even reframing the goal by breaking it down into more achievable chunks.

 Tip

Again you can support this by recognising the process, supporting the person's struggle to think through what they are doing and how they are doing it.

Peak performers are usually their own severest critics. They will often have unusual insights into themselves and how they are feeling, thinking and acting.

 Tip

Actively support the person in developing their insight and understanding about themselves, in achieving self-mastery.

[21] Charles Garfield (1986) *Peak Performers*, Avon Books.
[22] Maynard Leigh Associates (2010) 'Lighting the Fuse: Generating Peak Performance'.

High potentials can often benefit from detailed guidance on how to handle stress. First, they need to become more self-aware of their stress responses. Secondly, they may need practical support to achieve self-mastery that allows them to remain focused in the face of adversity.

 Tip

Self-awareness, managing conflict and a tolerance of uncertainty and ambiguity are all aspects of self-mastery that can affect peak performance. As a talent manager you may need to refine your awareness of these and how you can help others handle them at work.

Feel

In his now famous book, *The Inner Game of Tennis* (1974), Timothy Gallwey became an early advocate for the importance of understanding the inner world of the peak performer. In particular, he stressed the mental side of exceptional performance, the role of the mind, why we get nervous, and most importantly, how to deal with that nervousness, overcome it and perform at the highest levels.

 Tip

Help your potential peak performers by sharing your own understanding of the important role that their inner domain plays in a wide range of mental processes that affect achievement. Draw on your own experience, for instance for exploring with them issues such as attitude, resilience, self-awareness, self-confidence, persistence, alertness and presence.

Emotional intelligence is now widely recognised as a major factor underpinning various kinds of success at work, including leadership. Today's outstanding leaders understand and have mastered the use of emotional intelligence and failure to do so can prove severely career limiting. For example, Tony Hayward, CEO of BP at the time of the Gulf oil disaster, was widely criticised for his insensitive remarks including 'wanting my life back' which led to his premature departure from the top job.

Passion

This is one of the many characteristics that peak performers seem to share, regardless of the area of interest. It drives them to excel and they feel most alive when engaged at full throttle. In some ways it is a form of addiction, a passion to create oneself through work.

A number of private- and public-sector organisations – Ben & Jerry's Homemade, Southwest Airlines, Google and the UK's Dyson – incorporate passion as a key ingredient in their business strategies. They do it through communication, education, the environment they create, their policies and practices. It stems not from altruism, but because they realise that passion generates a constant stream of new ideas, innovation and builds huge personal commitment and loyalty.

Rooting out a person's passion begins with trying to connect them with what fills them with energy, what enables them to feel excited about reaching for their best. Be willing to use direct questions such as: 'What turns you on?', 'What excites you?', 'What can I do to help you succeed?', 'What's getting in the way of you being a star?' In other words, focus on the forces that motivate each person.

 Using passion

Steps to using passion are:

- **Start with the heart – discover what drives this person, excites and energises them.**
- **Clarify purpose – identify where the passion is leading and how it relates to the goals of the organisation.**
- **Define actions – agree on how the passion will be applied in what will be attempted.**
- **Encourage performance – ensure the person pursues their chosen path.**
- **Communicate – help share the excitement, gain attention and promote a sense of achievement.**
- **Persist – make sure the passion remains focused and driving peak perform- ance towards an agreed goal.**

In helping your potential peak performers explore their passion, make sure they come to recognise the distinction between being obsessed by the job, which can be dispiriting and hard to gratify, and pursuing their passion, which can give them satisfaction and fulfilment.

Act

If having a mission is a starting point for peak performance then those who go for it need to take the next vital step of responding with action – 'the click' that starts things moving. Follow through by helping them develop their skills, deliver on their commitment and be persistent.

Mastering of any skill is said to take at least 10,000 hours and there seem virtually no exceptions to this rule. In practice, most people can become reasonably good at a skill with an investment of 3,000 hours. What matters is not so much the numbers as seeing that your peak performers have plenty of opportunity to practise their skills and to receive regular feedback about the quality of that performance.

Persistence is when people press on regardless of their feelings and despite perhaps an urge to give up. It involves continuing to take action towards the vision, refusing to throw in the towel. Most people don't reach their goals because they give up too easily. The difference between people who accomplish their goals and those who don't is that despite the odds they keep at it! For instance, James Dyson so believed in his vacuum cleaner and making it successful that he simply refused to take 'no' for an answer.

Persistence also implies a willingness to learn from mistakes, being willing to adapt and change in the light of changing circumstances and a readiness to make course corrections. Traf-O-Data was the first company Bill Gates and Paul Allen started, back in 1972. They ran it for several years before realising it was not going to work. They corrected course and did rather better with Microsoft.

You may not be dealing with a James Dyson or Bill Gates in your organisation but you can pass on some of the lessons of persistence to your potential peak performers. For example, make sure they understand the difference between being persistent and being too obstinate to change.

There is strong evidence that physicality plays an important role in reaching peak performance. Focus your peak performers' attention on the value of staying fit and having a balanced life style. Even sedentary chess players do better when they exercise in preparation for tournaments. Exercise increases blood flow to the brain. The latter requires rich amounts of oxygen and glucose to fuel it and operate at peak efficiency. This leads to increased productivity, enhanced memory, better learning, improved moods and will power.

 Tip

Helping people at work reach their peak performance means making them aware of the role that health and well being play in reaching for their best. As some experts put it simply: 'The equation is very simple, strong body, strong mind.'

Removing the obstacles

When someone is not performing at their best be a detective and investigate the crime scene. Who or what may be causing the obstacles? These might include:

- a command and control approach to managing people
- making people conform to 9–5 hours, so they travel inefficiently in peak times

- presenteeism – insisting on seeing people in the office every day
- embroiling people in office politics and bureaucracy
- forcing attendance at lengthy corporate meetings
- giving people one size fits all cubicles, regardless of their needs or work styles
- an environment where it is hard to concentrate and easy to be interrupted
- not equipping people for optimal mobility and connectivity
- not using technology to best advantage
- not trusting people to make smart decisions about their best time and place to work
- counterproductive or adversarial relationships that drain energy and creativity.

Your own organisation's culture plays an important part in whether people hit their peak performance at work. As Mike Harris, founder of First Direct and Egg banking explains, his approach was 'to liberate energy, creativity, innovation and commitment' as a reaction against traditional large organisations, 'where the fundamental principle seemed to be a nose-to-the-grindstone culture where people are invited to trade in their quality of life for career advancement. Let's be clear – such businesses can produce high performance. I just wouldn't want anyone who I care about to work for them.'

Guiding people to peak performance is seldom routine. You are never safe in following traditional rules, strict schedules, generic methods and materials, or standard ways of assessing situations. To reach peak performance involves continuous experiment, even when everything seems to be working well.

Finally, if you are entirely wrapped up in reaching your own peak performance you are unlikely to be able to offer much support to someone else on the same road.

 Tip

Talent managing peak performance requires you to make space for the other person to excel, to see your own success as arising directly from theirs.

 Briefing lessons

- **Managing talent means helping individuals perform well and also to achieve exceptional or peak performance.**
- **High levels of engagement directly link to a number of important measures of company performance including work rates, sickness and absence, staff turnover and earnings per share.**

- As a talent manager concentrate on what will engage each of your direct reports, rather than risk becoming lost in the thicket of strategy and goals.
- Action that you can take to promote high levels of engagement includes management style, smart goals, coaching and performance reviews, motivation, talent identification, diversity and relating to Gen Y.
- The three top engagement drivers are a sense of personal accomplishment, confidence in senior management, and opportunities for training and development.
- The VIDI framework is another way of exploiting talent through promoting engagement by meeting four essential employee needs: to be valued, involved, developed and inspired.
- Many organisations are highly centralised with bureaucracies that result in rigid, top management styles. These tend to be controlling, conformist and monolithic. If this is happening in your organisation it will tend to deter engagement and hence work against peak performance.
- The essence of peak performance involves a combination of think, feel and act. In particular, passion is important and something that all peak performers seem to share. As a talent manager you need to become adept at rooting out people's passion using, for example, direct questioning. Steps to using passion are: start with the heart, clarify purpose, define actions, encourage performance, communicate and persist.
- Persistence in achieving peak performance is vital to success and is often the difference between those who ultimately achieve their goals and those who do not.
- Obstacles to top performance might include a command and control approach, making people conform to 9–5 hours, presenteeism, embroiling people in office politics and forcing attendance at lengthy corporate meetings.
- Other obstacles you should look out for in seeking to maximise the use of talent is to avoid one size fits all work cubicles, a distracting work environment, using technology incorrectly (including not equipping people for mobility and connectivity), not trusting them to make smart decisions about their best time and place to work, and poor relationships at work that drain energy and creativity.

How to measure talent

7

Introduction

If it is worth investing in talent management it is also worth discovering how effective it is. The three most common ways to evaluate it are:

1 obtain feedback from employees involved in talent management activities or their line managers
2 measure the retention of those identified as high potential
3 anecdotal observation of change.

For information about skills gaps or individual performance to work, it must be fed up and down the line. It should be freely available, open and transparent.

People are an organisation's main reason why it can compete and win. Products can be rapidly duplicated and services cheaply emulated. But competitors cannot so easily replicate innovation, quality of execution or in-depth knowledge. That people give an organisation its vital edge is now widely accepted, so consequently talent management has risen up many organisations' agendas.

As a way of radically improving workforce productivity and driving higher value for the organisation, talent management comes top of most executive's lists these days. Accordingly, individual managers and their more senior colleagues want to know whether their talent management is working, and if not why not. It therefore makes sense to demand convincing metrics and benchmark data to show the benefits of talent management. Those companies most committed to talent management tend to be the ones using the widest array of sophisticated metrics. Yet even the best players find it challenging to produce at an economic cost evidence of talent management delivering tangible benefits that outweigh the size of the investment.

In a 2009 report[1] on 20 companies with good talent management practices, Maynard Leigh found only one organisation, a leading UK bank, that could confidently declare, 'For every pound we spend on graduate training the bank receives £11 back in business benefits.'

Hewitt Associates in their webcast of 10 March 2009 stated:

Although many companies have invested in talent management technology, most still struggle to maximise engagement, performance, and the leadership pipeline. In addition, fewer than 10 per cent of these organisations utilise metrics that help them measure these objectives.

The view that talent management is cost effective often relies mainly on superficial statistics and assertion. As one sceptic of talent metrics quipped to us. 'If you don't think investing in your talent is worth it, try stopping doing it and see who's still there a year later.'

[1] Maynard Leigh Associates (2009) 'Talent Management at the Crossroads: How 20 of the UK's best employers are rising to meet the challenge of turbulent times'.

The Hackett Group's 2009 study[2] gathered both quantitative and qualitative data to show the pay-off from talent management. One of its most interesting if unsurprising findings was that those companies with the most mature talent management leaders achieved the best results. In other words, the more you do it, the better you become at it.

Talent management has been a persistent mantra in executive suites around the world. But when crisis in the form of turbulent economic conditions arrived, good intentions often altered abruptly. Numerous organisations resorted to lay-offs, sabbaticals, hiring freezes and pay cuts. Some slashed the training budget or at best trimmed it, while others eliminated entire departments.

A few insightful companies, though, cleverly navigated these tricky currents. By doggedly maintaining their commitment to talent, albeit sometimes in an amended form, they were able to retain their best people and even enhance their talent management capabilities.

Measuring your own input

You may rightly wonder how best to produce viable metrics about your own performance in managing talent. The solution is likely to come in the form of a trade-off:

- **Macro view**: Is it more important to have a diagnostic whose results can be compared against similar and dissimilar organisations for benchmarking purposes? Or
- **Micro view**: Is it more important to have a sharp, insightful instrument whose results can be used to improve your talent management and the business performance of your organisation?

The first view almost certainly demands a considerable investment over a lengthy timescale until evidence on the gains from talent management can be collated. The second view may demand a compromise on the depth to which you go to collect the information. Perhaps it is unfair to brand such investigations as 'quick and dirty', but they will usually lack the kind of academic rigour that severe sceptics require.

Whatever your choice it is probably best made along with colleagues and HR professionals. Your starting point for arriving at a viable talent management metric is clarifying in advance its specific aims. Without such clear expected outcomes it will be almost impossible to retrospectively 'prove' the benefits from previous talent management activity. And rather than trying to produce a metric showing the overall benefits from your talent management efforts, instead it may be more effective to focus on specific individuals whose talent you are managing.

[2] Di Romualdo, T. and others (2009) 'Hackett's Performance Study on Talent Management Maturity', The Hackett Group.

Line managers exert an important influence over many aspects of their direct reports' working lives, including their performance and levels of engagement. Therefore asking each direct report to comment on whether they are maximising their potential usually generates useful evidence on the talent management effort.

Employee attitudes can provide a basic metric that supports talent management practices. However, there is no substitute for understanding each direct report, how they experience their work situation, and then acting on the results.

A US study[3] into talent management metrics used by organisations found the top five most popular were

- talent retention rate (58%)
- time to hire talent (48%)
- cost to hire (41%)
- diversity statistics (38%)
- number of senior positions with identified successors (37%).

These probably do not fully reflect the additional costs of attrition from retraining, reinterviewing or reassigning people to different posts. Many organisations would rather not know these costs because they represent such a staggering amount of money walking out the door when talent is badly managed.

Organisations generally devote around 40–70% of their total operating spend on payroll and other direct employment expenses. Yet few make decisions about their people with the same discipline and confidence that they do about money, clients and technology. Putting it slightly differently, for all its known effectiveness, talent management seldom receives the attention it deserves and that includes identifying reliable metrics and acting on the results.

In well-established talent management systems there will usually be pre-developed reports and graphs covering the basics, such as turnover rates, average length of employment, and recruiting statistics such as the average time to hire, placement ratios, average length of stay for new hires and so on (see the table below).

Sample talent management metrics and benchmarks (all industries)

Acquisition metrics and benchmarks	25th	Median	75%
Rehire percentage (new metric)	3.7%	7.7%	13.7%
Referral hiring percentage	11.5%	20.5%	27.5%
Internal management hiring source	40.7%	50.0%	79.1%
Offer acceptance rate percentage	87.6%	91.0%	95.6%
Reward metrics and benchmarks	25th	Median	75%

Source: PricewaterhouseCoopers

[3] Human Capital Media (2010) 'Talent Management: State of the Industry Report', *Talent Management* magazine.

Yet while these are important, it requires more insight to fully grasp whether the talent management process is really working. More sophisticated metrics might include:

- **a competency gap index**: the difference between the skills the organisation needs to achieve its goals, and those that its current workforce possesses
- **an employee satisfaction index**: how happy employees are in their current jobs, and how likely they are to leave
- **a workforce confidence index**: that assesses employee perceptions of the abilities of the organisation as a whole – it provides insight into the reputation of the organisation among its workforce
- **ratio of external hires to internal promotions**: helps companies understand if they are properly cultivating their existing talent.

Since the exact mix of talent management practices are unique to each organisation so the relevant metrics will also vary greatly depending on the organisation's plans and goals.

Core skills

At its most basic, talent management exists to ensure there are enough people with the right skills for carrying out the organisation's current and expected business. This includes filling the skills gaps by recruiting externally and training internally. Too often, though, a suitable metric will be hard to find because there has been a lack of clarity about the actual purpose of recruiting. For example, is it for filling skills gaps, or about changing the skills profile of the organisation? Are new recruits needed to support the existing culture or help it move in a new direction?

Ideally, there should be a measurable and causal link running from business goals to talent management to recruitment strategies. Such a link can be difficult to pin down in numerical terms without adopting sophisticated measuring tools that often only the largest corporations can afford. Even the large ones can struggle to find the time and resources to pursue such metrics.

For example, when recruiting, companies may need to explore whether candidates have both the required skills and the right attitudes. There has to be a match, but how best to judge that? One familiar metric used is the extent to which individual's own values match those of the organisation's. Other metrics based around core skills might include evidence of leadership qualities, trustworthiness or customer care.

Compliance

The drive for compliance can also influence the choice and use of talent management metrics and not always in a benign way. For example, in a target-driven culture such as that found in many parts of the public sector and in some companies, the emphasis is strongly on having measurable results. These include the length of time it takes to answer a call, whether all legal compliance communication has been achieved, waiting times for services such as hospital operations in the NHS, and whether the correct amount of benefit has been paid to a claimant. Though reassuring, such box ticking sometimes comes at the expense of allowing talent to set its own goals and to take responsibility for delivering a good service.

Externally set targets by talent managers can force staff to meet goals which may not be a high priority for customers and can even be irrelevant to the organisation and its long-term aims. There is little point in cutting hospital waiting times, for example, if it means beds are made less often or that wards go uncleaned.

It is therefore important to keep in mind the bigger picture. Once established, an over-elaborate, compliance-related, talent management approach may become warped and too focused on certain metrics that ultimately do not lead to improved performance.

Competitive advantage

Since talent management has an enormous impact on the ability of an organisation to stay highly competitive, a key metric is one that shows talent management is indeed nurturing leadership, creativity and innovation.

In the global IT industry, for example, there is currently an acute shortage of graduate skills. Even corporate giants compete head on for a limited number of computer science graduates. In India the boom in IT has soaked up much of the available young talent. Talent-driven organisations like Microsoft must develop good talent management practice because it is only by attracting the right calibre of staff that they can compete. At Hewlett-Packard (HP), a priority in managing talent is being able to offer its IT engineers plenty of opportunity for international roles, fast tracking their career development and paying for them to take higher level professional qualifications.

Metrics that measure these activities are relatively simple to establish because the aim of talent management has been made suitably explicit.

Process improvement

Numerous diagnostic tools, often computer-based, exist to control and eventually show whether talent management as a process is working. One of the most complex systems developed by Carnegie Mellon University in New York, claims to 'set process improvement goals and priorities, provide guidance for quality processes, and a point of reference for appraising current processes.'[3] With the convoluted title of Capability Maturity Model Integration (CMMI), this heavily technological solution to talent management metrics is not for the faint hearted.

Rather more comprehensible is HP's approach called the HP HR Optimization Model, or the HROM. The model marries proprietary software with an almost philosophical viewpoint of integrated HR strategies. Some of these are based on industry standard definitions of learning and development, for example. Marcela Perez de Alonso, the Executive Vice President of Human Resources for HP, says HR no longer has to wait for business leaders to ask about workforce improvements; instead, HR can drive the conversation and show the data to support a business case for profit and productivity. She says:

We can go historically and say how this workforce looked a year ago, how it looks today and what we think it should [look like] in the future, given the business leader's goal.[4]

The Employee Value Proposition

This kind of metric works by showing whether there is a close alignment between the expectations of the organisation and the individual. For example, a particular metric might be one revealing whether employees feel well treated. Sometimes given the convoluted title of the Employee Value Proposition, it can help set the standards the organisation expects from its staff and in turn how they can expect to be treated. Such a metric will be collected in various ways, including the extent to which a person feels supported with performance management and coaching.

Once again such an approach begins and ends with the individual. For the metric to be viable an employee needs to be clear about what objectives the job demands, how they will be measured and what values they are being assessed against.

Recruiting on values

'Ours is a high performance culture, in which our values and principles are explicit and widely communicated,' claims the Corporate Director of Organisational and Human Development at Votorantim, Brazil's largest industrial conglomerate and the country's biggest cement maker. Talent management metrics can work particularly well in a strongly values-driven organisation like Votorantim where 'our

[3] www.sei.cmu.edu/cmmi
[4] P. Gallagher (2010) 'Inventing the Future of HR', Human Resource Executive Online, April.

key points of success include having clear diagnostics and engaging executives at every level.'

The UK Co-operative Bank presents another example of a values-driven organisation. It seeks a competitive edge by stressing its social values in its recruitment and marketing. Likewise First Direct bank recruits its phone operatives less on whether they know all about banking practice and more on whether they seem able to deliver on the bank's core value of relating well to its customers.

In values-driven organisations a typical talent management metric will be one measuring any mismatch between the espoused values of new recruits and those of the organisation. It is not unusual in using such a metric to uncover a gap between what people understand about a company's values and how they behave in their everyday jobs. Qualitative research can highlight such discrepancies and therefore provide talent managers with a metric about their effectiveness.

Nationwide Building Society: PRIDE

 *Nationwide Building Society refers to its values as PRIDE: **P**utting customers first, **R**ising to the challenge, **I**nspiring confidence, **D**elivering best value and **E**xceeding expectations. This easy to recall acronym provides a solid benchmark against which to compare the values of potential staff.*

Conducting research and workshops with middle managers can be another route to measuring discrepancies between values and how they are applied in an organisation. For instance, external consultants working alongside middle managers can help determine how far they 'live' the values and whether they actively use them in managing people.

Johnson & Johnson

 Long before anyone coined the expression corporate social responsibility Robert Wood Johnson, Founder and Chairman of US pharmaceuticals company Johnson & Johnson, developed a set of company values in 1943. The company established health and healthy relationships at the root of its industrial relations policy. It was pure values-driven talent management in which the company pledged to put the needs and well-being of the people it served on an equal footing with its employees.

Referred to as the Credo, the company describes its values-driven culture in this way:

We are responsible to our employees, the men and women who work with us throughout the world.

Everyone must be treated as an individual.

We must respect their dignity and recognise their merit.

They must have a sense of security in their jobs.

Compensation must be fair and adequate, and working conditions, clean orderly and safe.

We must be mindful of ways to help our employees fulfil their family responsibilities.

Nor are these just idle words on a wall chart. The whole credo is built into how employees talk. In conversation about work-related matters staff can be heard to remark disapprovingly, 'That's very "off-credo".' The company empowers staff to challenge whenever they see people acting against what they see as its core values. Rather than being an empty set of words, it is absolutely how people are expected to behave.

With such clarity about the purpose the Credo creates a whole mindset and provides a solid foundation for viable metrics on whether talent management is working or not.

Employee engagement

There is now powerful and hard to refute evidence that high levels of employee engagement affect significant aspects of a company's performance, from profits to sales, from retention rates to absenteeism. Therefore it makes sense to measure engagement levels as an indirect way of assessing talent management's effectiveness.

Numerous definitions of engagement exist, some more elaborate than others. The one we like best is that engagement is:

When employees feel able to commit to the organisation so as to perform to their full potential, in particular to give exceptional discretionary effort. We can best sum up the latter as: going the extra mile.

Given the importance of such behaviour talent managers may choose to measure

- absolute levels of employee engagement
- the outcomes from high levels of engagement.

Absolute levels

Absolute measures of engagement present a straightforward picture of engagement including the elements that together create engagement. For example, as discussed earlier, Maynard Leigh uses four key variables (see Figure 7.1).

Figure 7.1 The four variables

Source: © Maynard Leigh Associates.

Using a simple employee questionnaire a company can acquire information about each of these variables. The output provides a picture of the impact of its talent management practices by assessing levels of engagement (see Figure 7.2).

Figure 7.2 Levels of engagement

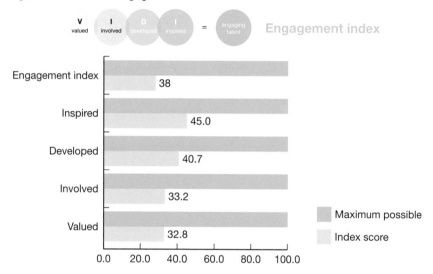

The popularity of employee surveys suggests that most HR directors believe that these can demonstrate the value of talent management strategies. One HR director in a service sector company admitted that he focused his entire talent management budget on boosting employee engagement. However, what ultimately counts is that the metrics are put to good use and acted upon.

Outcomes from engagement

Rather than rely on an absolute measure of engagement (see above) to assess the effectiveness of talent management activity, it may be better to explore indirect outcomes. For example, 'pulling a sickie' is a persistent feature of the UK's public sector. High sickness rates therefore provide a picture of something going seriously awry with employee engagement, and by implication talent management.

According to the 2009 UK MacLeod and Clarke study[5] on engagement, beneficial changes in financial performance, customer care, sales, innovation, profit, attrition rates, wastage and sick leave can all be influenced by high levels of employee engagement. All these variables therefore lend themselves to relatively easy forms of measurement.

Making sense of development and metrics

Many companies invest heavily in programmes that try to develop their talent, whether as a privileged elite or on a more inclusive basis. The annual cost and effectiveness of these plans are yet another route to pinning down the success or otherwise of talent engagement practices. However, development plans that merely consist of a list of courses to attend, or appraisals that give almost no indication of where the employee sees themselves in the future or how they might get there are all too common, and tend to be unreliable metrics.

Recession, in particular, has focused minds on talent: What is it worth to the company?, What value is the talent management programme adding?, What aspects of the programme produce the best return?, and so on.

A large UK retail bank measures the value its graduate trainees add to the business by calculating the extra revenue created by a graduate in a revenue-generating role. It extrapolates from here to include the total number of graduates, to give a total return to the business. The bank also compares this performance with a control group of non-graduates in other parts of its business. As its talent manager explained:

> We separate out what is cost from what is return, to produce a cost to income ratio. For every pound we spend on talent management we see multiple returns in the form of additional sales.
>
> Our training programme therefore shows a dramatic return to the business.
> In a climate where the competition is cutting back I know where I'd be investing my money.

Leadership development is an important area in which organisations invest sometimes heavily to develop existing talent. Deciding whether the development is worth it can be difficult since it may take several years before the evidence of successful leadership emerges. For example, CEO Jack Welch was renowned for saying that he spent a significant amount of his time ensuring that there were credible successors in the GE talent pipeline. Yet it was several years before this pipeline was tapped to produce his heir, and more years before it became clear that the chosen one was delivering on his potential.

[5] David MacLeod and Nita Clarke (2009) 'Engaging for Success: Enhancing performance through employee engagement', A report to Government, Office of Public Sector Information, Information Policy Team.

There may be many kinds of development underway at any one time: leadership talent, expertise talent, entrepreneurial talent, and so on. It is important to clarify with some precision the aim of development so as to create a viable metric.

Metrics based on individuals

Employees with personal development plans tend to be more engaged at work than those who do not. So yet another source of metric is identifying the impact of each person's development. This might include measuring the extent to which a person works well in a team, communicates, persuades, relates to others, works across organisational boundaries, shares knowledge, networks, and so on.

Talent pool

The size of the talent pool and whether it is working provides yet another talent management metric through monitoring the proportion of vacancies that are successfully filled from within the organisation. Another view of the success of talent management is whether the organisation can maintain a pool of people with critical skills that are difficult to obtain in the labour market. For example, certain specialist engineers may be in short supply so a talent segment may be defined around this group specifically to ensure such skills are available for internal growth.

Britannia Building Society: high performers

 Adrian Powell, Head of Britannia's leadership and people development, says:

> *We identified a group of 40 people last year who we see as high performers. We put them through a development centre where assessment is the prime focus. The next step is to match that talent pool against the key strategic initiatives of the business. It enables me to manage the risks – have we got the right people now – the talent population to meet the strategic direction of the organisation?*

Lloyds Banking Group: the talent pool

 Jacqueline Davies, recent Group Head of Talent and Executive Resourcing at Lloyds, took a robust view of the company's talent pool and the accompanying succession planning:

> *We need to understand a lot more about vital roles and gaps. It depends on how you do it. If it's in terms of critical roles you build up a better diagnostic around what you need to build for the future of the organisation. It gives you insights. Succession planning is a good place to start asking where we need to go. We need to get better at understanding what the data is telling us. We need to look at all sorts of succession planning data – how deep is it? How much talent do we have?*

Metrics in perspective

It is clear from the above that in assessing talent management's success there is no single magic metric that will 'prove' it is working well. Almost certainly you will need an array of measures that together can provide insight into the success or otherwise of talent management.

Organisations with mature, effective talent management practices enjoy significant bottom-line gains, including earnings that are 18% higher than companies that have less advanced practices. Therefore there is considerable incentive for sorting out what metrics will be used regularly to underpin talent management activity.

Desirable though metrics are for supporting the talent management effort it is sensible to be aware of just where these can go wrong. The best practitioners are better at increasing overall employee engagement, achieving faster recruiting cycle time and ensuring greater linkage of talent management to business strategy.

One approach to metrics is the use of technology and HR professionals everywhere seem to be falling in love with it. But how useful are such systems and what software solutions are right for your organisation? More significantly how do these often expensive technical solutions actual produce a good return on your investment?

Without becoming immersed in the arcane world of computerised talent management systems, it is enough to know that simplicity is often a safer bet than complexity. Secondly, such systems are best suited to medium to large organisations. An important gain from using these software approaches is that they force you to be data-driven, i.e. evidence-based. Wishy-washy hunches and impressions mainly stay outside the system.

Keeping the system simple sounds obvious, yet as a survey by the New Talent Management Network of its roughly 2,000 members reported in early 2010 'the simplicity and accountability of talent practices scored low in most companies, but emerged as huge drivers of effectiveness when present'.[6] Finally, while an apparently integrated control system that brings together all kinds of human resources data may look attractive, in reality it may prove complicated to implement and ultimately fail to deliver the kind of answers talent managers need.

If you decide a computer-based talent management control system is for you, make sure it really is as easy to use as Google, Amazon and other consumer sites. Most of the clunky systems we have seen are strictly designed for geeks and are doomed to failure. You do not need a manual to use Google. The same goes for any talent management system: it must be intuitive and useful from day one.

Whatever metrics you finally settle on, make sure they are driven by simplicity, accountability and transparency. These have been shown to predict the effectiveness of various talent management practices. This is particularly so in the areas of talent reviews and succession planning.

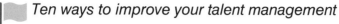 *Ten ways to improve your talent management*

1 Avoid metrics for the sake of metrics, make sure yours align closely to business goals.

2 Establish a process for deciding what you consider success.

3 Seek to be able to answer the question: Is my talent management working well or not?

4 Make sure chosen metrics drive intended action, not just provide information.

5 Pay particular attention to levels of employee engagement and ways to measure it, not just once but regularly.

6 Narrow down the talent metrics to a manageable few and probably not more than two or three.

7 Use a metric to show whether succession planning within your own area of influence enables mainly, if not exclusively, internal recruitment.

8 Consider establishing a metric showing employee retention rates within your sphere of influence.

9 Benchmark your local retention rates both across the organisation and with those of comparable organisations.

10 Track talent development and performance to make smart decisions about talent.

[6] www.newtmn.com

Common errors in pursuing TM statistics

- **Metrics for the sake of metrics.** The metric chosen needs to be closely aligned to what managers and leaders will accept as evidence of effective talent management practices.
- **Too many metrics.** Over-enthusiastic collection of data can swamp any ability to make sense of the mass of information, leading to inaction.
- **Inadequate follow-up.** Metrics are at their most useful when managers use them to trigger action.
- **No record of methodology.** It is important to have adequate documentation showing what each metric is meant to indicate, and how it will be monitored, collected and analysed.
- **Underestimating data collection problems.** Some metrics prove far more tricky to collect than at first expected, with layers of complexity to unravel in making sense of them.
- **No benchmark.** Metrics that cannot be compared against some kind of norm or standard will soon lose their attraction.

 Briefing lessons

- Higher-performing organisations are more likely than lower performers to have devised metrics strategies. Those that excel at talent management are nearly twice as likely to actively use workforce metrics strategies.
- The main choice for metrics is between long-term, rigorous and often expensive systems that accumulate evidence and cheaper, less robust, yet often more useful approaches.
- The four master steps to developing talent management metrics are: analyse existing workforce metrics, decide what the new system is meant to achieve, devise and implement a plan to improve metrics over time, and know how to bring the eventual metrics to life.
- Various issues that influence the selection of talent metrics include: core skills, compliance, competitive advantage, process improvement, the Employee Value Proposition (EVP), recruiting on values, employee engagement levels and employee development programmes, metrics based around individuals and size of talent pools.

- There is a trend towards using technology to define and provide viable metrics. But while these systems try to integrate a large range of management processes they are often complicated and only suitable for medium and large organisations.
- On the whole the best approach is likely to be one in which the metrics and processes chosen are transparent, simple to understand and accountable. It is better to adopt just a few salient metrics rather than generating large quantities of data that will never be followed through and used.

How to talk about talent management

8

Introduction

Talent is the ultimate competitive advantage. Organisations therefore experience a strong strategic reason to manage it well. Yet, many line managers avoid the implications, remaining unconvinced about this kind of investment in time and resources.

For example, a 2006 study by Ashridge Consulting and the Chartered Management Institute[1] showed that more than half of all line managers are resistant to talent management processes. Other studies around the world have indicated extremely varied rates of buy-in across different managerial groups.

Consequently, there is a need to think carefully about how you choose to talk about talent management. If, when asked 'How does talent management affect you?' four out of five employees reply 'not me', as indicated above, then finding the right language to explain its benefits is clearly important. Putting it slightly differently, you may need to develop astute ways of talking about talent management so that its essential message comes across and appeals to your audience.

If talent management is to thrive in your organisation, it needs to attract different groups, not just a few senior policy makers. For people to buy into it they must recognise tangible benefits. These might include higher profits, more productivity, greater innovation, improved working conditions, greater work satisfaction, a chance for promotion, the opportunity for formal development or more rewarding work and so on.

Even with most of your strategic leaders and a small number of high potentials supporting the talent management idea, it still may not mean that your organisation pursues it in a sustainable way. To give it staying power talent management needs grass roots support and in large organisations the commitment of middle management. Although around half the organisations in the UK seem to use some form of talent management system, over a third of managers say that theirs do not and the rest do not know.

Getting clear on the meaning

When you talk about 'talent' what do you actually mean? One useful working definition is:

> *I mean by talent everyone in the organisation, since everyone can make a difference to our organisation's performance, either immediately or longer term by fulfilling their potential.*

Equally you might choose to be more focused on skills and say:

> *I mean by talent those people with critical skills which have become difficult to recruit.*

[1] Ashridge (2006) 'Developing Future Leaders: The contribution of talent management'.

Making a case for investing in talent management can be tricky unless you are clear about what it actually means. Talent management does not have to be about either the whole workforce or just senior leadership. In many organisations there is a step-by-step development approach for the workforce in general, with more specific and centralised interventions for those with leadership potential. It may therefore be easier to talk instead about specifics such as succession planning, learning and development, career advancement, identifying high potentials, attrition rates, engagement and so on.

So talking convincingly about talent management means devising clear messages for different audiences, and using different approaches:

 Different audiences   *Different approaches*

- **High potentials**
- **Board level and senior managers**
- **Line managers**
- **Front line staff**
- **Other stakeholders, such as shareholders**

- **Turn your talk into questions**
- **Talk about a story**
- **Talk about the processes**
- **Talk about engagement**
- **Talk about unlocking potential**

Different audiences

Talking to high potentials

High potentials – your most valued talent – will usually be on the receiving end of the talent management system, so may need little persuading about its benefits. Yet they too need to understand what resources will be available and when and where this investment is likely to lead. In other words, high potentials may want it spelled out how the talent management process will support their personal growth and career prospects.

The more specific the message about what talent management can deliver in the way of a career progression the greater the likely commitment of high potentials.

 Tip
Talking about 'where you are likely to be in 18 months' time' in terms of career can be an attractive way of both retaining and attracting talent.

Talking to board members and senior managers

The phrase 'talent management' sounds important, rather strategic and even exciting. As one HR director told the Institute for Employment Studies: 'It plays well as a term in the boardroom.'[2] However, while board members and senior managers may readily buy into the philosophy behind talent management, they may still require convincing that an actual investment will bring short- and long-term benefits.

Frame your talk about talent management as practical issues with which senior managers can readily identify. For example, pose questions like: Are there enough potential leaders in the pipeline? What is staff attrition costing? Can talent give us a real competitive advantage?

A Deloitte poll[3] revealed that while 65% of companies are nervous about losing high potential employees and critical talent to competitors, only 35% have updated their talent retention plans. The evidence suggests that almost one in three employees is actively searching for new jobs and nearly half is considering leaving their current ones. The situation is worse among younger staff with only 37% of Gen X and 44% of Gen Y employees planning to remain with their current employers.

 Tip

By presenting this kind of information in a dramatic way you can readily win the attention of otherwise sceptical senior policy makers, especially if you back it up with the actual financial cost of, say, staff attrition.

Offer senior managers clear, action-based messages such as:

- Did you know that according to the recent government report on engagement that a 1% increase in employee commitment can lead to a monthly increase of 9% in sales. Isn't this worth doing something about now?
- We need to take retention seriously now, let's not just wait for the recession to recede.
- Loss of trust amongst staff is a national issue and we're probably not immune to it. Let's fix a clear strategy for restoring trust levels, otherwise we'll pay the price in attrition rates and low levels of engagement. Talent management can help us achieve this.

[2] V. Garrow and W. Hirsh (2009) 'Talent Management: Issues of focus and fit'. Institute for Employment Studies.
[3] 'Critical Disparities between Employer Perceptions and Employee Turnover Intentions', a 2009 Deloitte study.

- We need to do more than measure people's levels of engagement. We also need to invest in daily measures that show us we're winning people's discretionary effort.

- Our leaders and managers need to feel equipped to inspire people and know what it takes to re-energise both individuals and teams.

- If we want behavioural change to lead to improved levels of performance we must avoid grabbing at more short-term cuts. The process of managing talent and unlocking potential takes time. We need a proper investment of resources.

Another way of framing your arguments about talent management to appeal to this high-profile group is to talk about the advantages of adopting a more joined-up approach to utilising the organisation's people. For example, you might make the point that talent management can help make sense of the vast amount of people data that the organisation collects at considerable cost: 'It can provide us with a 'dashboard' for how well the resources are being used'.

This senior group may also respond to some limited metrics that convey the benefits of talent management, such as the cost of high staff attrition rates, or the gains from improved levels of performance.

Similarly, it may be easier to gain their attention with a question such as 'Where are our future strategic leaders going to come from?' or 'Is it good management to divide up our workforce into advantaged and disadvantaged groups – a few we invest in and the majority we don't?' But ultimately the most persuasive argument may come down to simple stories and anecdotes about how talent management works and the hard to refute assertion that 'Talent management is definitely for us!'

Talking to line managers

Line managers have a pivotal role in talent spotting, providing development opportunities, performance management, giving feedback, and coaching and supporting those who carry the burden of being labelled as 'talent'.

Since it is line managers who must make the talent management system work, it is hardly surprising that many remain sceptical about its benefits. In talking to these people focus on down to earth issues such as:

- 'Do you want to improve individual performance?

- 'Do you think retaining talent is an issue here?'

- 'Is handling your most talented people a challenge?'

They will also tend to respond to the prospect of protecting their most talented team members from being poached by external or internal predators. Explain how talent management offers ways to move this issue onto a rational system for sharing talent for the general benefit.

Talking to front line staff

The term 'talent management' will probably not convey a lot to most front line staff and may even cause anxiety. For example, the Institute for Employment Studies reported in 2009[4] that:

> We found that mentioning talent management in many organisations makes many people nervous. They start to wonder, 'What do we mean by talent? Talent for what? If I am talent, what will managing me mean? And if I am a manager will I need to tell some people that they are not as talented as they thought they were?'

As a CIPD report[5] about what it feels like to be talent-managed put it:

> It is increasingly important to understand what employees really value in terms of talent management opportunities and to use their feedback to improve the offerings.

Become familiar with the sort of benefits people experience when they are being talent managed and you will find it easier to talk to them about the whole process. Figure 8.1 shows some recent findings. This suggests that it makes sense to talk to them about issues such as developing new skills, promotion, creating challenging experiences, being more productive and greater career opportunities.

Front line staff, though, may care little for anything called talent management, particularly if it comes down to channelling scarce resources to an elite of star performers. To avoid that perception, you may need to show that some activities are for all and some are tailored to specific needs. For example, at the National Audit Office activities for all talent pool members included an external assessment centre, mentoring, master-classes, action learning and personal development planning. Tailored activities for the few included carefully selected secondments, further education, challenging projects and new job roles.

Explain talent management in highly personal terms, such as how the process will directly affect individuals, for example in ensuring they have meaningful work or encouraging them to fully use their potential. Describe the development programmes that they will be able to access. People also need to see there is

[4] See note 2.
[5] CIPD (2010) 'The Talent Perspective: What does it feel like to be talent-managed?', Survey Report.

Figure 8.1 Benefits that people experience

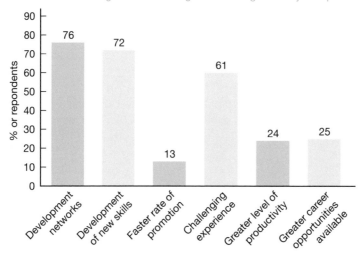

Which of the following benefits of being talent-managed have you experienced? (%)

Source: The Talent Perspective: what does it feel like to be talent managed?, CIPD (2010).

a systematic and transparent approach to unlocking their potential, rather than idiosyncratic responses by individual line managers. So talk about the benefits of reviews, assessment centres and new ways to identify talent.

 Tip

Explaining that 'you are part of our talent pool' is an important way of under-pinning high engagement and may create self-fulfilling prophesies that one will grow with the organisation.

Talking to other stakeholders

Other stakeholders, such as shareholders, may see little gain from money spent on developing people, unless this is also linked to achieving specific company objectives, such as improving profitability.

Likewise, unions may come to support talent management if the investment in people is transparent, is spread equitably throughout the organisation and is likely to lead to tangible gains in remuneration.

Tip

Again the different interests mean it is essential to frame the arguments in ways that appeal to each group.

Different approaches

Turn your talk into questions

You may find that it is useful to focus people's interest in talent management by presenting the issue in the form of some basic questions, such as those shown in the box.

 Talent management questions

- Do our recruitment programmes attract our future managers?
- Do we know which employees are ready for management positions?
- Can we identify inspirational or potentially inspirational leaders?
- What will be our staffing needs in five years' time?
- Which employees are at risk of leaving, what can we do to keep them?
- Do we have the right skills mix to achieve our goals?
- What will our future leaders need in the way of specific skills and attributes?
- Should we limit development to a few high potentials or spread it more widely?
- What is the current attrition rate in the organisation and what is it costing?
- What is the level of engagement in the organisation?
- How do we raise engagement levels to attract maximum discretionary effort?
- Does our remuneration strategy actively support talent?
- What metrics do we rely on to manage our talent?

You do not need to have all the answers to these questions. They are merely triggers to get people thinking and talking. They enable you to raise important issues and push for an effort to find the answers, and from there to promote talent management as a whole.

For example, you might explain:

We tend to assume that our high potentials are enthusiastic about our company and are highly engaged people. Well, unless we're a complete exception, we could be kidding ourselves. Did you know that the national evidence suggests that one in four of our top people could be planning to leave us within the year? Or that one in three would admit to not putting all their effort into the job. That could be costing us a small fortune!

Or try this:

> *According to national research one in five of our employees probably has entirely different aspirations to what we have in mind for them. Don't you think we should find out what they are thinking, in a systematic way?*

Or consider this approach:

> *Let's not just equate our current high performers with future potential. Did you know that research shows that 70% of today's top performers lack the essential attributes for their success in future roles? For us that could mean the bulk of our current talent investment is being wasted on individuals whose potential is not all that high. Shall we talk about it?*

Organisations spend countless hours, energy and money maintaining systems that capture key employee data. Talent management offers the ultimate opportunity to put that data to effective use. So in raising these questions you are, in effect, demanding evidence that these systems are actually useful, beyond being a bureaucratic exercise in data collection. What you are seeking is the creation of a unified story that will help streamline business processes, and which will drive decision making, planning and analysis.

What is your company's take on talent? Do not be fobbed off by people telling you 'there is no such approach here' or that this is something new. Saying 'we don't use or need talent management' may be a valid philosophical stance, but it tends to stop people thinking about it intelligently.

Your company's approach to talent may be buried in the culture somewhere, but it is going to be there. It is like air conditioning, you may not see the pipes and the machinery but you know when it's working and when it's not.

Talk about a story

This is how the CEO of the ROK building company described his efforts to transform his organisation, create a shared vision and in effect introduce better talent management practices.

> *When I started this journey people thought I was mad and the Board were not universally enthused. But I knew that without getting the workforce fully engaged and committed the company would die. Instead of which it was reborn.*[6]

Another way of talking about talent management and gaining buy-in is to use stories, anecdotes and exemplars that bring the message to life. For example, the gains from ensuring high levels of employee engagement are now well established. There are countless published lively tales about what such levels achieve, such as lower attrition rates, higher levels of profitability, more innovation, better safety at work and so on.

Often the success stories come from research or other organisations. Be willing to use these to get your message across. They may be straightforward endorsement for talent management, inspiring case studies where people have implemented talent management systems, or evidence that challenges the status quo.

Talk about the processes

Yet another way of talking about talent management is to do so in terms of the various processes that it uses, such as succession planning, reviews, development programmes, diversity and so on. For example, the succession process can help everyone, while still allowing a focus on high potentials and whether these will provide the skills and leadership needed for the future.

Legal & General: sharp focus on succession planning

 Legal & General plc has changed tack and brought succession planning sharply into focus. Here is how Group HR Director Elaine MacLean talks about it:

> *In previous years a lot of our development budget was spent on middle managers' skills – getting them through externally accredited Institute of Leadership and Management (ILM) programmes. The spending was on core skills and practical operations-based courses. Now the focus is on future requirements – succession planning. In our organisation we have a lot of key talent that is critical for the roles they do, such as actuaries.*

The corporate message that the company is willing to invest in high flyers can be a useful talking point, but it may also mean explaining that there has been a rethink about priorities. Here is what one talent director of a FTSE 100 company said:

> *The recession has helped us prioritise. We now run one grad scheme where in the past we ran three. We now get more bangs for our bucks.*

Similarly, you might instead talk about the development process that underpins talent management in your organisation. For example, here is how Group Learning and Development Manager Carole Teacher of civil engineering consultancy Mott MacDonald Group Ltd talks about their new professional development programme to boost engineers' commercial skills:

---

[6] David MacLeod and Nita Clarke (2009) 'Engaging for Success: Enhancing performance through employee engagement'. A report to Government, Office of Public Sector Information, Information Policy Team.

We didn't have resources to develop everyone as that would mean a programme involving 800 people a year ... people must show they will benefit from the programme and demonstrate they are motivated to be included. We're trying to help people move their careers on inside the company rather than outside.

Atkins: a more holistic approach to talent

 HR Director, Group Talent Management, Brian FitzGerald of the engineering consultancy Atkins, talks of a 'more holistic approach to talent'.
The recession has made the company talk more openly about focusing on deploying talent effectively and on redeploying talent within the company:

Individuals don't have to aspire solely to becoming a business manager in order to do well. We have three career routes to ensure individuals are valued equally if they have technical, business or project management expertise. You can have a career, not just a job in Atkins.

Talk about engagement

While experts argue about the precise meaning of employee engagement, it is now a central plank of talent management. Engaged employees are people willing to go the extra mile, to put in discretionary effort. It is a contribution they do not have to make, they voluntarily choose to do so from a sense of commitment and being inspired to perform, often beyond their own expectations.

Over 100 studies worldwide have shown the close linkage between engagement and performance. Be ready therefore to talk about engagement as part of making your case for talent management. Refer to the undeniable evidence that high levels of employee engagement directly and favourably affect a company's bottom line. The UK government report on engagement,[7] for instance, found that over a 12-month period companies with high engagement scores secured a 13.7% improvement in net income growth. Those with low engagement scores saw net income decline by 3.8%.

Or talk about the fact that 'high levels of engagement are strongly linked to higher levels of innovation'.[8] Similarly, 'engaged employees take less sick days than the engaged, an average of 2.69 sick days per year versus 6.19'.[9] And of, course, engagement affects staff retention because engaged employees are far less likely (87%) to leave the organisation than disengaged ones.

An IES study[10] indicated that 'a one per cent increase in employee commitment can lead to a monthly increase of nine per cent in sales'. Similarly, a Hay Group report[11] concluded that engaged employees outperform their peers in less captivating environments by 15–30%. As for customer service, Nationwide found significantly higher scores for customer experience in areas of high engagement. The Co-op reported evidence of direct correlations between high levels of engagement and store business performance.

There are broadly two types of employee engagement: transactional and integral. The former is less desirable than the latter and companies tend to be in one group or the other. This may influence how you choose to talk about talent management in your own organisation.

Transactional and internal

The transactional group of companies regards employee engagement as essentially a set of tasks or targets. Here, employee engagement, and by extension talent management, tends to be compartmentalised, treated as an add-on and not integral to the business. For these companies, talent management remains essentially a set of discrete, unlinked activities.

By contrast, the integral group of companies puts talent management centre stage. Such companies regard employees as the essential cast for developing and delivering an outstanding business performance. It is a mindset, in which employees, including their values and behaviours, reside at the heart of strategy development and of high levels of performance.

Based on CIPD experience, three out of four organisations pursuing engagement strategies treat it as transactional, while one in four treats it as integral to talent management.

If yours is a transactional organisation, your key people will probably view engagement and talent management as only useful if it gets quick results. This approach sits uneasily with the amount of culture change that might be needed to make engagement effective and talent management generally worthwhile. Successful companies find that pursuing engagement in an integrated way is worth the effort. For example, Towers Perrin found that of the many drivers of engagement 'the one that was rated as the most important was the extent to which employers believed that their senior management had a sincere interest in their well-being.'

Maynard Leigh Associates has similarly argued that what produces high levels of engagement is that managers make employees feel valued, involved, developed and inspired (VIDI).

---

[7] Ibid.
[8] Ibid.
[9] Ibid.
[10] See note 2.
[11] Hay Group (2010) 'Playing the Numbers Game: How good is your leadership'.

Talk about unlocking potential

Finally, yet another effective way of getting talent management onto company agendas is by referring to the value of unlocking people's potential. Companies are increasingly moving away from the concept of the war for talent which treats it as a scarce resource. It no longer seems sensible to engage in the battle to recruit from a relatively small pool of so-called talented stars performers. Instead, talent is increasingly seen as coming from diverse sources because tomorrow's companies will need to be adept at discovering, engaging and leading every ounce of individual and collective capacity in people.

The new concept within talent management, and one we strongly advocate throughout this book, is therefore about how to tap into the full potential of the workforce. As one industry leader publicly put it in 2002:

If we can get a disproportionate share of the most talented people in the world, we have a chance of holding a competitive edge.

Conclusion

Talent is undergoing a transformation. We live in uncertain times of global recession, a changing economic landscape, demographic pressures and the ability of talent to vote with its feet.

Rather than technology, talent is emerging as the defining factor of organisational success. In talking about it you may need to refer to the many, not just the few. Your message needs to be about the benefits from releasing people to be themselves to achieve their potential, working in an environment that represents their values and recognising them as individuals.

Organisations are becoming more anarchic, harder to manage, less predictable. We are learning to treat them not as machines, in which we can predict what will happen if you pull a particular lever. Your reason for talking about talent management is that it is a response to a changing business environment and a move towards being more active about development and performance management. You might choose to put it in these simple terms: 'If we grow our people, we will grow our company.'

Briefing lessons

- In order to be effective, talent management needs to attract different groups, not just a few senior policy makers. It must become something that everyone can sign up to, not just the bosses.
- You must be able to explain the tangible benefits your people stand to gain. These might include improved working conditions, greater work satisfaction, a chance for promotion, and the opportunity for formal development or more rewarding work. In turn your company should reap the reward of higher profits, more productivity and greater innovation.
- When explaining the benefits of talent management use stories that bring to life what it can deliver in the way of business performance and personal benefits.
- Many people and organisations strongly resist the whole idea of talent management. Learning to talk about it convincingly and persuasively involves finding ways to articulate the issues and communicate the benefits, so people understand what's in it for them or their organisation.
- Tailor the message to different audiences: using different approaches.
- Use a variety of approaches to get across the talent engagement message.

[PART THREE]

Intervention

Executive intervention

9

Introduction

Is your organisation fit for the 21st century? Once, the secret of success was to keep getting bigger. Size brought valuable economies of scale. It justified ever more mergers and acquisitions, most of which, though, failed to deliver the promised business benefits. Numerous forces are reshaping the economic playing field. They include a heady brew of globalised markets, skills shortages, demographic trends, corporate governance, business strategy, increased competition, digital technology and expectations about the role of organisations in society.

The name of the game is no longer 'size matters'. Instead, it is becoming 'How can we become talent-driven?' Talent is taking centre stage in organisations because it is the only reliable way to survive a constantly turbulent and unpredictable environment. Consequently, the shape of the 21st-century successful organisation is already in view. Talent is central to its core purpose whether through horizontal networking, the need for continuous improvement, the demand for high performance teams or the need to scale learning.

20th-century firm	21st-century firm
Vertically integrated	Horizontally networked
Top-down leadership	Distributed responsibility
Build the ultimate product	Continuous improvement
Gain efficiency	Scale learning
Hoard information/build IP	Share information
Experts	Learning new skills
Lone hero	High-performance teams
Security	Transparency
Push	Pull

Source: Reproduced with permission from 'Leveraging the Talent-Driven Organization' (2010) Richard Adler (rapporteur), The Aspen Institute.

What are the make or break decisions?

Being a manager implies continuous interventions that draw the best from staff, inspiring them to go the extra mile, and finding the next generation of leaders from the biggest possible gene pool. Today, every manager is now a talent manager. Faced with the challenges of complexity, uncertainty and ever-increasing competition, business leaders have begun to appreciate that talent management offers real help in generating profit and turning around situations where there is potential for serious failure.

Each organisation will have its own definition of talent and will identify a set of procedures that ensure it attracts, retains, motivates and develops the talented people it needs now and in the future. Here are some of the make or break decisions.

What definition of talent will you use?

Defining what you mean by talent can help you form a talent management strategy that meets the needs of your organisation. A definition we have found helpful is:

Talent consists of those individuals who can make a difference to organisational performance, either through their immediate contribution or in the longer term by demonstrating the highest levels of potential.[1]

As a manager of talent you need to link talent management processes with business goals. These processes include:

- sourcing critical skills to meet short- and long-term business goals
- building a high-performance workplace
- strengthening the organisation's performance and its ability to compete
- providing a framework for recruiting and developing talent
- encouraging a learning organisation that constantly adapts
- enhancing the organisation's brand by becoming an employer of choice.

Almost certainly you will need to prioritise. Choose what is most urgent within your organisation. Defining talent management will help you prioritise the actions you need to take.

For example, Zurich HR Director Chris McCormack explains that the company has finessed its strategy 'to take account of the present economic context. Rather than reducing our focus on our high talent population, we have sought to make efficiencies in our talent management spend. We continue to make sure our talent management strategy is strongly linked to business objectives.'

Decide what your organisation's talent needs are – now and in the future

In large organisations this inevitably proves to be a complex, long drawn out process in which succession planning, talent pools and the likely availability of suitable recruits may all need to be considered. What matters at this stage, though, is the decision to systematically assess talent requirements, in terms of both demand and supply.

[1] CIPD (2010) 'Talent Management: An overview', revised July.

Part of this decision will be an analysis of exactly who the organisation wants to retain, who the high potentials are and who will need to be developed. While you may already do this informally, the point of a talent management system is to adopt a more systematic way of obtaining this information, using methods that are fully transparent. Nailing down who has the potential to progress and then establishing programmes that ensure their development can be time consuming. There are numerous support tools available, ranging from specialist talent management software to solutions like the McKinsey nine box grid than can help make the process more rational.

Recruit only the best

Yet another key decision is the choice about the quality of those you recruit. Where specific types of talent are scarce, you may need to pay close attention to the basis of recruitment. For example, do you recruit only the best, or people who are 'fit for purpose', i.e. those that are 'good enough'? You cannot afford to leave this kind of decision solely to the HR professionals; they need clear guidance on what the organisation should be looking for and why.

Who should we develop?

Who should the organisation be developing? Is it everyone employed or instead a chosen few, the most talented or those with the greatest potential to excel or become tomorrow's leaders? These are heady choices and have implications far beyond the initial decision.

A common corporate view is to prioritise succession planning. Boards do this because it seems easier and more economic to focus on a few individuals. The results are also easier to measure, both in terms of the value a person can bring to the brand and the damage that a lack of future leaders can inflict.

Developing the next generation is a legitimate choice but it demands a pro-active effort, usually supported by HR professionals. It may include assessment centres, psychometric testing, devising fast-track stretch tasks for talented individuals and then tracking their progress. It is a labour-intensive activity but it is relatively easy to establish a measurable return on investment.

Seek opportunities to develop talent

One of the key functions of any leader is to help people develop their unique talents. It is also the core of talent management.

Global organisations usually seek opportunities to move key employees around the business. For example, the decision by BP to send Richard Dudley to manage its operations in Russia gave him ideal experience to expand his diplomatic skills. Later they proved much needed, when he replaced the company's existing CEO, the reputation-damaged Tony Hayward.

Moving people around to develop their talent takes active decision making, it does not just happen naturally. Those suitable for this kind of experience have to be identified, the specific learning required must be determined and the opportunity for placement must be found in an organised way. When such opportunities are found they can help foster a unified culture and uncover skills that can help the organisation. One HR director of a FTSE 100 company which had reorganised and merged various business units in response to the recession explained that this gave senior management more responsibility for setting business objectives: 'This was our largest organisational restructure. If you can't find a development opportunity around that, then something's wrong!'

Encourage openness and transparency

Talent management systems work best when their procedures and target audience are public knowledge within the organisation and even beyond it. Employees need to understand where they fit in in terms of the organisation's development efforts and to see how they can become part of it.

One of the advantages of deciding to make the whole process open and transparent is that it provides a common language for talking about development, talent and making decisions about investing in people. Succession planning, for example, can be on a more systematic basis and individual careers can be mapped out more clearly. One HR director told us: 'We don't go into specifics of succession planning but we need to establish a shared view of what talent is. What are the opportunities and how we can work together to develop that.'

Use line managers as talent ambassadors

If you decide to use line managers as talent ambassadors you will taking an important step in enrolling a key stakeholder group in the talent management process. Even if your organisation has an HR team, it cannot micro handle all the complex issues around exploiting talent. In many situations talent management devolves either formally or informally to line managers.

Line managers must take on the talent management task because they are closest to where the talent is and can see firsthand the contribution it makes to performance, and where day-to-day decisions that affect talent are actually made. Zurich, for example, has created what it describes as a 'talent management culture' in which all line managers receive training as talent managers.

When is my intervention needed?

There will be numerous times when you might intervene to promote talent management. So what are the main touch points that are most likely to need your attention? Intervention helps you develop a talent culture within your organisation.

But intervention must be timely and linked to outcomes. Here are some useful interventions.

Promote the process and generate a supportive environment

In a recessionary climate issues arise that may have no easy answers. For example, many managers have spent much of their time in full cut-back mode and devoted little time to nurturing or harvesting talent. You may need to intervene to ensure more attention goes on supporting the talent that can drive renewal and growth.

Boost employee engagement

This issue has now penetrated the higher echelons of all but the most antediluvian organisations. Because high levels of engagement are so closely linked to individual and corporate performance there is plenty of justification for focusing on this critical aspect of talent management.

Ensure that talent receives the attention it deserves. For example, line managers may need practical help with performance management, giving feedback, having effective conversations, coaching and generating high levels of engagement.

Treat each employee as an individual

This is part of the secret of successful talent management but not every line manager finds it easy to put into practice. Your own modelling and showing the way may be as important here as any direct intervention you choose to make.

Identify and develop new leaders

Depending on your seniority you may need to limit your interventions to setting standards, agreeing benchmarks and strategy. Some senior leaders, though, see it as important to take a personal interest in identifying and developing new leaders and get satisfaction from their involvement. For example, Peter Brabeck-Letmathe, Nestlé CEO from 1997 to 2008 and Chairman of the Board since 2005 argued that, 'I consider succession planning to be the most important thing of all. I will have achieved nothing if my successor doesn't turn out to be at least as successful, and hopefully even more successful, than myself. That's the sign of a good leader. If the company only does well as long as you're at the helm, and then collapses after you go, you weren't much of a manager.'

What questions should I ask?

In deciding how to intervene to support talent management in your organisation, there are naturally many questions you might ask along the way. Asking them is a lot easier than finding the answers, but a few well-aimed questions can sharpen up your choice of how and where to intervene.

Try answering these questions as they apply to you, and in doing so follow where they lead, talking to others in your organisation to explore the possible answers:

- Am I clear about what I mean by talent?
- Does my view of talent fit with how the rest of the organisation views it?
- Do I know the main boundaries of my talent management role?
- How exactly can professional and specialist staff assist me in managing talent?
- In managing talent, what key features of the external environment do I need to take into account?
- Is our talent pipeline working well and what might be making it more effective?
- How do my talent management practices compare with others in my organisation?
- What tools can I use to identify the right talent, assess potential and promote employee engagement?
- How do I measure the success of my talent management?
- How could I help make us an employer of choice?
- Are my mentoring and coaching skills adequate for enhancing performance?
- Do I take my Gen Ys seriously and am I fully engaging them?

What levers should I pull?

In pursuing talent management you may understandably feel that there must surely be levers you can pull to make things happen. Unfortunately a mechanistic view of the organisation is no longer credible. There are no sure ways of affecting change through taking single actions or pulling the equivalent of an organisational lever. Organisations are organic and complex adaptive systems, in which any intervention can trigger unpredictable and sometimes unfavourable results.

It is more appropriate to consider 'How can I most effectively influence change?' Concerning talent management, this is likely to be through intervening in a number of key areas such as:

- promoting innovation, growth and breakthroughs in performance
- linking talent management to business strategy (see above: make or break decisions)

- pay and prospects
- communication
- awards
- corporate social responsibility (CSR)
- training and development
- gender balance and diversity.

Promoting innovation, growth and breakthroughs in performance

Here the intervention that will have most impact is likely to be in helping others to achieve these aims. For example, you may need to eliminate blocks to creative thinking that could impede innovation. Or you could find that only your direct involvement in introducing a system of performance management will ensure that it gets off the ground.

Pay and prospects

These are organisational quicksands that can rapidly swallow up even the most efficient manager. Rather than becoming immersed in the arcane world of remuneration and reward systems, stay focused on the critical issue of incentives that will help retain talent.

Above a certain level, financial rewards cease to act as a motivator. For those with talent, pay for example may be far less valued than prospects or an opportunity to do something new or creative.

Even in a recession talent still has choices with surveys showing that up to a third of people labelled as 'high potentials' are actively considering moving to new pastures. High potentials continue to walk out the doors of organisations because they do not feel the development process is mutually beneficial, and this is almost regardless of pay levels.

Communication

Communication can be a considerable source of influence in pursuing your talent management aims. Effective talent managers, for example, will share with people how the business is performing in the downturn or upturn. Potential sources of conflict such as the need for redundancies or restructuring should be communicated sooner rather than later.

In considering your executive intervention look for mechanisms that allow you influence both at a macro and micro level. An HR manager of a home counties computer software company told us:

> We have monthly management meetings which give staff information on profit and turnover so that people can see how the business is doing. It's designed so that people can feel management is listening.

A London advertising agency designates Friday as a day for talking. The HR director says:

Once a week we have Friday drinks in our office kitchen and relaxation room. It creates the right environment for people to be engaged and stimulated. The key thing is open communication. We open the floor to questions and challenges.

We take our employee engagement survey very seriously. It's not just a process. We are very conscious of the very strong link between how we treat our customers and how we treat staff. We survey all staff on a quarterly basis and the results are fed to the board. Each of the directors will then go to his or her division and discuss the results with their team before deciding what to do.

Although staff surveys provide vital feedback on employee engagement and can be a useful tool in talent management, they are no substitute for actually talking to people and directly affecting how they think and feel.

Awards

Within your sphere of activity ensure there is a commitment to celebrating success. Public moments in which people's successes are shared and celebrated can have a disproportionately large impact on change. These vital occasions reinforce the talent management culture and help move people further in the direction that you want them to go.

Given the limited opportunities for firms to pay bonuses in a recessionary climate, an awards ceremony can be highly effective in recognising talent and its achievements. It is also a chance for everyone to come together and have a good time. HR Director of Talent Management at BskyB, Sarah Myers, says:

We now have our annual awards ceremony for staff. Anyone in the company can vote for anyone and our CEO and the group of chief executives select the winners. We also have special awards linked to departments. The staff working in sports vote for their annual 'Golden Balls' award and our entertainment department has their equivalent of the Oscars, it's called the 'Grafters'!

Corporate social responsibility (CSR)

Another area of influence is through interventions around corporate social responsibility. Research shows that high potentials in particular are motivated by organisations that take their social responsibilities, such as charitable activity, seriously and have a strongly ethical culture.

Insurance group Zurich, for example, had 80 teams doing community challenges across the UK in 2008 and Chris McCormack, talent management tsar of the group, commented:

Something we're proud of is engagement with the community. In the area of corporate social responsibility we've being a player for a long time. Zurich Community Trust has driven a lot of activity. It provides significant funding for programmes and work such as the Marie Curie Trust and the Calvert Trust which is a hospice organisation. We have funded an eye hospital in Gujerat and the Association for Physically Disabled People in India. Our CSR programme is a brand within a brand.

IBM employs its most valuable resource – its technology and talent – to create innovative programmes that assist communities around the world. Since the inception in 2003 of the company's On Demand Community over 145,000 employees and retirees have registered and performed almost 10 million hours of volunteer service around the world.

CSR activities directly and indirectly influence how organisations are perceived by employees, particularly those whose potential they most want to influence.

Training and development

This core element of any talent management system is one you can and should influence. It is also highly vulnerable to reductions during recessionary times. However, companies that are seriously committed to managing talent generally take the opposite view. In our survey we found not a single company had axed its training, although several were making small-scale cuts and adjusting priorities.

A poll in 2010 of global high potentials by Talented Psychology Consulting revealed 'organisations which responded to the recession by limiting opportunities for challenge and creativity and who played it safe have damaged their ability to thrive as recovery returns, by alienating the very employees who create superior value.'[2]

One talent manager told us:

We understand that people are building a career with us. You come in as a graduate or at any point in your career and continue to grow. We are a dynamic organisation, we make sure people are always growing and learning. We invest in learning. We want to keep people stimulated.

If you choose to intervene in this area, issues you might explore include:

- What is our T&D effort costing?
- Is it producing a worthwhile return on investment?
- Does it deliver the skills we need to grow the organisation?
- Do our high potentials value the T&D experience?

[2] Karen Ward (2010) 'Talent Management in Recession and Resurgence', Ashridge Consulting.

- Is there a real dialogue between individuals and the organisation about whether the T&D programme meets mutual needs?
- Who decides on which people receive training and development and is the process transparent?
- How aligned is the T&D effort to the organisation's current business goals?

Gender balance and diversity

No need to be altruistic about wanting to affect the gender balance in your organisation. Let simple business sense prevail! Gender balance correlates with better corporate performance, better return on investment, greater innovation and more stock price resilience in crises. In its 2009 survey of women leaders, McKinsey showed that 'women more than men demonstrate five of the nine types of leadership that improves organisational performance'.[3] So using the organisation's female talent makes absolute sense.

Yet in 2010, the UK Financial Reporting Council called for a better gender balance on UK corporate boards to avoid 'group think'. And while most (89%) American companies have at least one woman at executive committee level, only 32% of European companies and 18% of Asian companies do. Whatever the legislation, women are set to make a significant impact on male-dominated careers. In science, engineering and technology, the number of UK women undergraduates rose 55% in the past 10 years as against a rise of just 29% for men.

While there seems no real difference between male and female leadership effectiveness, Northwestern professor Alice Eagley, who specialises in the subject of gender differences, finds a number of differences in the leadership styles of business men and business women.

Men's styles	Women's styles
Task-oriented	Team players
Autocratic	Democratic
Command-and-control	Transformational
Punishment-oriented	Reward-oriented

Discrimination in the workplace is most easily identified by the gap that persists between men and women's pay. In spite of legislation the gender pay gap is still hovering at 20%. Some might argue that the pay gap is caused not by discrimination but by market forces. In his controversial report *Should We Mind the Gap?*, J.R. Shackleton, Dean of University of East London Business School, argues that while women gravitate towards degrees in the arts, education and nursing, men

[3] McKinsey (2009) 'Women leaders, a competitive edge in and after the crisis'.

head for higher-paid careers in business, law and medicine. Men's higher salaries reflect, he says, greater stress and the risk of being made redundant. Professor Shackleton adds: 'Forcing employers to increase pay is an extremely costly business and means job cuts for men and women.'[4]

The gap starts with gender stereotyping and low aspiration – something which schools and colleges should address. The five 'Cs' – clerical, cashiering, caring, catering and cleaning – attract the most women and are where the lowest paid jobs are found.

There is evidence of female attitudes starting to influence management. Women managers see themselves far more in a nurturing role.[5] They see their job as managing individuals whereas men believe managing is all about task – getting the job done at any price. So what can talent managers learn from this? And how can they show a more even-handed and more integrated approach when dealing with men and women?

Having women role models in senior management who mentor their younger colleagues can boost the numbers applying for management. Senior women have often had to overcome discrimination. Those who have had to take time off to bring up a family will probably have fought hard for family-friendly working practices such as the right to flexible working, job sharing and being encouraged to make a phased return to work after maternity leave.

RM: women-friendly policies

 Women-friendly policies can have a big impact as Abingdon-based educational software company RM has discovered. A third of the graduate intake and a quarter of front line staff are women: women occupy at least three senior board positions. HR manager Deb Self says:

We find that flexible hours and offering women with children at school the chance of term time working adds up to a better work–life balance.

The more women are promoted to senior positions within a company the less likely they are to tolerate inconsistency. At KPMG the gender balance is evenly split but equality peters out the higher you rise in the organisation. Just 14% of profit-sharing partners are women. The firm is investing in women's networks and coaching and preparing women for partnership. For the past few years KPMG has had an equal pay review, a major step towards fairness and transparency.

---

[4] J.R. Shackleton (2008) *Should We Mind the Gap?* Hobart Paper 164, Institute of Economic Affairs.
[5] Women's Executive Development Program (2004) 'Senior Women Executives and the Cultures of Management', University of Technology, Sydney.

Encouraging a better gender balance

- Demand targets for recruiting women to management.
- Managerial and leadership shortlists must include women candidates.
- Monitor to ensure women are getting their fair share of opportunities.
- Ask women in senior management to mentor younger colleagues.
- Set up and publicise a women's network.
- Create women role models within the company.
- Offer family friendly workplace policies including flexible working hours and career flexibility.
- Promote on merit, but discriminate positively when candidates are equally qualified.
- Provide opportunities for development.
- Identify what is 'unique about your organisation' that would be of interest to potential women job applicants.
- Publicise positive results of employee surveys, flexible working conditions, and commitment to training and development.
- Ensure appraisal systems are gender neutral and performance focused.
- Offer personalised career paths to retain the best talent.
- Ensure performance evaluation systems neutralise the impact of parental leave and flexible working arrangements.
- Encourage gender diversity indicators in executive performance reviews.

How do we know we've succeeded?

If you are a senior executive, you will probably be expected to play an active part in deciding to what extent the talent management system is:

- delivering on its promised benefits
- favourably affecting business goals.

These decisions need to be arrived at jointly with HR professionals, who may be steering the entire talent management system. Their views should be balanced with those of section heads, supervisors and others dealing with the day-to-day reality of the management of talent. However, you can only know if the organisation is succeeding with its talent management process if clear goals have been set for it. So make sure you know what these goals are, and the metrics used to assess them.

Apart from any formal metrics, seek out some of the indirect signs of success. For example, to what extent are more people being given responsibility and encouraged to perform to a high level? Research confirms that where this occurs people are more likely to be productive and with higher profits for the organisation.

Another sure sign is the existence of high levels of engagement and leadership impact. These may also form part of the goals for the talent management system. For example, most global surveys show poor levels of engagement in organisations and low levels of trust in leadership. Seek out the scores for your organisation.

The public sector is increasingly adopting talent management policies and its *People Survey*[6]*,* run by the Cabinet Office, covers some 350,000 civil servants. In 2009 a snapshot of key variables among its staff showed:

- 90% were interested in their work
- 85% were treated with respect by the people they work with
- 83% felt they could rely on their team when things get tough
- 79% believed everyone in their team worked together to improve the service they provide
- 78% of staff agreed that their manager was open to their ideas.

The results also pinpointed where improvements were needed. 'By establishing this survey', said Sir Gus O'Donnell, Head of the Civil Service, the organisation has shown that 'it is taking its responsibility to ensure staff are properly engaged very seriously. It gives us the evidence we need to build on our strengths and tackle our weaknesses.'

As the Civil Service's senior executive, O'Donnell therefore has the answers he needs as to whether or not its talent management system is delivering. The challenge of bringing about change 'is not going to be an easy or quick task, but it is at the heart of raising productivity. Strong employee engagement has a strong connection with productivity and improved employee health and wellbeing. Improving engagement is crucial to delivering better quality public services and better value to the taxpayer and will be one of the key leadership challenges the Civil Service faces in the next decade.'

Finally, you can make a reasonable assessment about the success or otherwise of the talent management system by tapping into informal networks in your organisation. What, for example, are people saying about it on the intranet, on blogs and other social media? What do your line managers tell you about how the system is working and do they feel confident with their own talent management role?

[6] Civil Service People Survey (CSPS) Benchmark Results 2009.

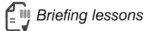 *Briefing lessons*

- There are many opportunities for executive intervention in support of talent management. In fact the playing field is so large that it is important to narrow it down to tackle the key issues and their implications.
- The first major intervention is to decide whether the organisation needs a formal talent management system and, if so, agreeing on what 'talent' will mean within it.
- Another important intervention is making sure there is a clear understanding of what the organisation needs in the way of talent and to identify current and future gaps. Other make or break decisions include: linking talent to business goals, recruiting only the best, deciding who to develop, seeking out opportunities to develop talent, encouraging openness and transparency, and using line managers as ambassadors.
- When to intervene requires you to consider various touch points most likely to affect talent and how it is managed. These include actively fostering a talent culture, ensuring more attention goes on supporting talent that can drive renewal and growth, focusing on levels of engagement, making sure the support system for talent provides practical help, treating each employee as an individual, and fostering improved performance and developing new leaders.
- In deciding how to intervene executives may need to ask many questions along the way. It is suggested that you try answering 12 questions as they apply to you and then following where they lead into the organisation.
- It would be convenient if there were some reliable levers to pull in pursuing talent management but it is probably more appropriate to consider how you can most effectively influence change. This is likely to be intervening in a number of key areas such as: promoting innovation, growth and breakthroughs in performance, linking talent management to business strategy, pay and prospects, communication, awards, corporate social responsibility, training and development, and gender balance and diversity.
- In choosing to intervene in the area of training and development, to consider: What is the T&D effort costing?; Is it producing a worthwhile return on investment?; Does it deliver the skills needed to grow the organisation; do high potentials value the T&D experience?; Is there a real dialogue between individuals and the organisation about whether the T&D programme meets mutual needs?; Who decides on which people receive T&D and is the process transparent?; and How aligned is the T&D effort to the organisation's current business goals?

- In considering an intervention in the area of gender balance and diversity there is overwhelming evidence that companies that achieve this perform better than ones that do not. There are many ways of encouraging a better gender balance and some of these are listed separately.
- How do you recognise whether the organisation is succeeding in its talent management efforts? Check first whether it is delivering on promised benefits, and secondly whether the system is favourably affecting business goals.
- Apart from using formal metrics there are also various indirect signs of success that one might watch for. One is that more people are being given responsibility and encouraged to perform at a high level. Another is the existence of high levels of engagement and leadership impact. Generally, engagement levels tend to be low and so too are levels of trust in leadership.
- It is also possible to assess the success or otherwise of the talent management system by tapping informal networks, both within and beyond the organisation. This includes asking line managers whether they think the system is working well and whether they feel confident about their own talent management role.

[PART FOUR]

In depth

Additional resources

10

- Articles and reports

- Weblinks

- Books

- Podcasts

- Software

- Courses

- Consultants

Articles and reports

2002

'The War on Talent? Talent Management under Threat in Uncertain Times', CIPD.

'The War for Talent: Building a strong talent pool to drive business performance', McKinsey and Co.

'The Talent Myth' by M. Gladwell, *The New Yorker*, 22 July, pp. 28–33.

2004

'The risky business of hiring stars' by B. Groysberg and others, *Harvard Business Review*, 1 May.

2006

'Trends in Human Capital Management: The emerging talent management imperative'. A Knowledge Infusion White Paper.

'Developing Future Leaders: The contribution of talent management', Ashridge Business School.

'Talent Management in the 21st Century: Attracting, retaining and engaging, employees of choice', *World at Work*, Towers Perrin.

2007

'Talent Management: Understanding the dimensions', CIPD.

'Engagement is Not Enough' by Jeremy Starling, Hr Zone.

'How to manage key talent' by S. Brittain, *People Management*, Vol. 13, No. 12, 14 June.

'How to measure the success of talent management' by A. Likierman, *People Management,* Vol. 13, No. 4, 22 February.

'Talent: Strategy, management, measurement', Research into Practice, by C. Tansley and others, CIPD

'Building an Integrated Talent Management Strategy', Economist Intelligence Unit.

2008

'Engaging employees to drive global business success', Insights from Mercer's What's Working™ research.

'Talent management for the twenty-first century' by P. Cappelli, *Harvard Business Review*, Vol. 86, No. 3, March.

'Talent Management's Impact on Employee Engagement', Headlight Communications.

'Talent Management: Design, implementation and evaluation', CIPD.

'Common Sense Talent Management: Twelve fundamental principles for increasing workforce productivity', by S. Hunt, Success Factors, Inc.

2009

'Engaging for Success: Enhancing performance through employee engagement', A report to Government by David MacLeod and Nita Clarke, Office of Public Sector Information, Information Policy Team, Kew, Richmond, Surrey TW9 4DU.

'Talent Management at the Crossroads: How 20 of the UK's best employers are rising to meet the challenge of turbulent times', Maynard Leigh Associates.

'Talent Management: An overview', CIPD.

'Fighting back through talent innovation: talent management under threat in uncertain times', CIPD.

'The Talent Imperative' by DeAnne Aguirre and others, Booze & Co.

'A to Z of Generation Y attitudes' by Alison Maitland, *Financial Times,* 18 June.

'Q12® Meta-Analysis: The relationship between engagement at work and organizational outcomes' by James K. Harter, Gallup, August.

'Talent management's role in a time of recession' by N. Murphy, *IRS Employment Review*, No. 927, 13 August.

'Talent Management: Issues of focus and fit', by V. Garrow and W. Hirsh, Institute for Employment Studies.

'How Gen Y and Boomers will reshape your agenda' by S. Hewlett and others, *Harvard Business Review,* July–August.

'Key Findings from Hackett's Performance Study on Talent Management Maturity', The Hackett Group, HR Executive Insight, obtainable on application: www.thehackettgroup.com/tmmaturity

'The talent innovation imperative' by DeAnne Aguirre and others, from *Strategy+Business*, Issue 56, Autumn.

'Threading the Talent Needle: What global executives are saying about people and work', Deloitte.

'Talent Reframed: Moving to the talent-driven firm', Richard P. Adler, The Aspen Institute.

2010

'Leadership lessons from India', by P. Capelli and others, *Harvard Business Review*, March.

'Leveraging the Talent-Driven Organization', Richard Adler (rapporteur) Communications and Society Program, The Aspen Institute.

'The Talent Perspective: What does it feel like to be talent-managed?', CIPD Survey report, Summer.

'How to keep your top talent' by Jean Martin and Conrad Schmidt, *Harvard Business Review,* May.

'The Rules of Engagement' by the Training Foundation.

'Opening Up Talent for Business Success: Integrating talent management and diversity', CIPD, March.

'Talent Engagement', Maynard Leigh Associates.

'Talent Management: An Overview', CIPD.

'How to link reward and talent management', *People Management*, February.

'Talent Management Survey 2010: Executive Summary', by R. MacKinnon and James Christopher, TalentQ.

Weblinks

The strategic logic of diversity by Lord Browne, Speech on 19 June 2002 at Women in Leadership conference, Berlin: www.bp.com/genericarticle.do?categoryId=98&contentId=2002278

Talent management: Issues of focus and fit by Valerie Garrow and Wendy Hirsh, Winter, at: www.entrepreneur.com/tradejournals/article/print/192352084.html

Talent Engagement Review: www.talentmanagementreview.com/

People Management: www.peoplemanagement.co.uk/

CIPD: www.cipd.co.uk/default.cipd

Free Management Library: managementhelp.org/hr_mgmnt/hr_mgmnt.htm

HR Review Update and newsletter: www.hrreview.co.uk/

Talent Management online magazine: www.talentmgt.com/

Talent Management network at Linkedin: www.linkedin.com/nhome/

HR Zone: http://www.hrzone.co.uk/

Talent Management network: network.talentmgt.com/

Talent Management in recession and resurgence, Karen Ward, Ashridge Consulting: www.ashridge.org.uk/(search under Talent Management)

Talent Psychology: http://talentpsychology.com/

Books

Bibb, Sally 2010 *Generation Y for Rookies,* Marshall Cavendish.

Blass, Eddie (ed.) (2009) *Talent Management: Cases and commentary*, Palgrave Macmillan.

Borensztejn, Herve (ed.) *Growing Talent: A corporate duty,* Marshall Cavendish Business, 2010.

Cannon, J.A. and McGee, R. (2007) *Talent Management and Succession Planning*, CIPD toolkit, CIPD.

Cheese, Peter, Thomas, Robert J. and Craig, Elizabeth (2007) *The Talent Powered Organization: Strategies for globalization, talent management and high performance*, Kogan Page.

Foster, Steve (2009) *The Big Book of HR: Inspiration and possibilities in contemporary human resources*, Northgate Arinso.

Gallwey, W. Timothy (1986) *The Inner Game of Tennis*, Pan Books.

Garfield, Charles (1986) *Peak Performers: The new heroes of american business*, Random House.

Goldsmith, M. and Carter, L. (eds) (2010) *Best Practices in Talent Management: How the world's leading corporations manage, develop, and retain top talent*, Pfeiffer.

MacLeod, David and Brady, Chris (2008) *The Extra Mile: How to engage your people to win*, FT Prentice Hall.

Parry, E. and Urwin, R. (2009) *Tapping into Talent: The age factor and generation issues. Research into practice*, CIPD.

Silzer, R. and Dowell, B.E. (2009) *Strategy-Driven Talent Management: A leadership imperative*, Jossey Bass.

Saville, Prof. Peter and Hopton, Tom (2009) *Talent: Psychologists personality test elite people*, Saville Consulting.

Podcasts

'It's 2010: Where is your retention strategy?' Deloitte, available as podcast and transcript download at www.deloitte.com

Various podcasts on Talent Management: www.aquire.com/downloads/podcasts/

Podcast #1 – Sylvia Vorhauser presents 'Integrated talent management'; Podcast #12 – Kevin Wheeler presents 'The future of talent management' and others at www.pageup.com.au/resource_download_podcasts.htm

'The modern corporate learning organization: How informal learning and talent management is transforming corporate training', recorded on 12 August 2009: www.sumtotalsystems.com/index.html (see Resources>Podcasts)

Talent Management: Eliminating Complexity, Adding Value, hosted by: Allan Hoving: www.humanresourcesiq.com/podcastlist.cfm?id=1

Talent Management University of Westminster, Annual HRM Conference 2010: www.westminster.ac.uk/schools/business/news-and-events/news/news-items/talent-management-2010

IQPC 13th Annual Talent Management Summit, 2010, various: www.talent managementevent.com/Event.aspx?id=318010

Software

Human resource management systems focus on the prosaic side of HR such as payroll, employee records and benefits administration. Talent management software has evolved from these core HR services to provide on-demand sub-scription-based services to automate, document, standardise and overall improve how organisations manage talent. The more comprehensive suite of tools deal with

- performance management
- goal management
- compensation management
- talent acquisition/recruiting
- learning management systems
- career development
- succession planning.

These can potentially help companies take a more strategic approach to dealing with talent.

Many vendors can configure their software to meet a broad range of require-ments. Having a clear set of goals in mind will select the right vendor(s) for your business needs. Many vendors have evolved over time to offer a full suite of solu-tions. However, most started with a focus on a particular area/functionality such as recruiting, performance management, learning and so on, which makes them more mature in those areas.

Some useful comparative sources include:

- Talent Management Systems 2010, Executive Summary. Bersin and Associates research report, published September 2009, available as download at www.bersin.com
- Top 10 Talent Management Software, 2010 edn. Profiles of the leading talent management software vendors, 47 pages, available as download at: www.Business-Software.com

- Comparisons and sources of TM software, available as download at: www.2020software.com
- A comprehensive study of customer experience with talent management systems, 2010, available as download at: www.bersin.com

Courses

Many large and small development organisations offer workshops and learning experiences on talent management. For example, there are over 300 courses listed under talent management at www.emagister.co.uk/talent_management_courses-tps236547_2.htm

Usually short courses of one or two days, talent management courses are normally run as in-house or bespoke programmes, adapted to meet the specific needs of a particular organisation.

In-house programmes may focus on strategy, on the psychology of talent management or on the more detailed practical activity of managing talent such as:

- how to design and manage career systems and assessment
- understanding processes that develop talent
- tools to identify future potential in employees
- learning how to develop processes and activities that promote potential within individuals
- how to design management development programmes
- making a business case for introducing emotional and spiritual intelligence as key competency frameworks for managing talent.

There is also a Postgraduate Certificate in Talent and Career Management validated by the University of Surrey, available from the CIPD.

Consultants

Virtually any aspect of human resources management can be 'converted' to some aspect of talent management. Consequently the route to selecting a suitable consultant is strewn with traps for the unwary. For example, there are a multitude of freelance contractors and consultants but no real way, apart from word of mouth recommendations, of choosing a suitable provider.

Trade associations such as the Management Consultancy Association tend to favour the large companies, which may not always be an ideal solution. There are also many smaller specialists in virtually all the areas that make up the talent management focus including

- developing strategy
- designing processes and systems
- retention and reward systems
- career management
- assessment systems
- succession planning
- leadership
- cultural awareness
- interview preparation
- choosing dedicated talent management software.

A comprehensive guide on choosing a management consultant by the Management Development Network, though aimed at the voluntary sector, spells out the essential stages and some of the key questions to pursue: www.mdn.org. uk/choosing.htm

Index